MATTIE LEE PRICE

# THE FORGOTTEN
# GEORGIA WONDER

# MATTIE LEE PRICE
# THE FORGOTTEN
# GEORGIA WONDER

DONNA LEE DICKSSON

**Mattie Lee Price**
The Forgotten Georgia Wonder
Donna Lee Dicksson

ISBN 979-8-9861747-2-3  PRINT
ISBN 979-8-9861747-3-0  EPUB

Cover Design: riverdesignbooks.com
Cover photo: Cabinet Card Photo of Mattie Lee Price
courtesy of The Warren Raymond Collection.

Published by Donna Lee Dicksson
www.dicksson.com

# — Dedication —

♡

*I am forever grateful.*
*Grandma Jessie Blair*
*& Friend, Marika Leth*
*–Angels*

# — Acknowledgements —

Thanks to my husband Peter for everything. Cousins Tina, Linda, and Anita: Your research and corroboration made Mattie's story possible. Family matters. To the army of volunteers around the world that make book, photo, and newspaper archives available online, Mattie's family is eternally grateful.

A special thanks to the ladies of the "Stilesboro Improvement Club" for preserving the Academy for future generations.

A big thank you to the circus and freak collectors, museum curators, and other total strangers who lent a hand in uncovering Mattie's story. We found genuine consideration and assistance wherever we enquired.

A special thanks to all those who listened to me talk endlessly about Mattie Lee Price.

Mattie. Thank you. I wouldn't be here without you.

*Thank you!*

*Donna Lee Dicksson*

# — *Author's Note* —

To maintain authenticity, I have retained the original text in the advertisements, articles, quotes, and other published references, complete with their incorrect spellings, punctuation, and grammar.

# Contents

Acknowledgements . . . . . . . . . . . . . . . . . . . . . . . . *vi*

Author's Note . . . . . . . . . . . . . . . . . . . . . . . . *vii*

Chapter One . . . . . . . . . . . . . . . . . . . . . . . . . *1*

Chapter Two . . . . . . . . . . . . . . . . . . . . . . . . *13*

Chapter Three . . . . . . . . . . . . . . . . . . . . . . *25*

Chapter Four . . . . . . . . . . . . . . . . . . . . . . . . *32*

Chapter Five . . . . . . . . . . . . . . . . . . . . . . . . *46*

Chapter Six . . . . . . . . . . . . . . . . . . . . . . . . . *56*

Chapter Seven . . . . . . . . . . . . . . . . . . . . . . . *67*

Chapter Eight . . . . . . . . . . . . . . . . . . . . . . . *83*

Chapter Nine . . . . . . . . . . . . . . . . . . . . . . . . *92*

Chapter Ten . . . . . . . . . . . . . . . . . . . . . . . *104*

Chapter Eleven . . . . . . . . . . . . . . . . . . . . . *119*

Chapter Twelve . . . . . . . . . . . . . . . . . . . . . *129*

Chapter Thirteen . . . . . . . . . . . . . . . . . . . . *147*

Chapter Fourteen . . . . . . . . . . . . . . . . . . . . *153*

Chapter Fifteen . . . . . . . . . . . . . . . . . . . . . *166*

Chapter Sixteen . . . . . . . . . . . . . . . . . . . . . *172*

Afterword . . . . . . . . . . . . . . . . . . . . . . . . . *181*

The Last Word . . . . . . . . . . . . . . . . . . . . . . *187*

About the Author . . . . . . . . . . . . . . . . . . . *189*

# — Chapter One —

*A*LL KIDS HAVE A MOMENT when they think what they are seeing is just too good to be true. Time stops and mouths gape. You remember that happening, don't you? Take a second. Go ahead. Close your eyes. Think about it.

It was July 1957. I was five. The Carson & Barnes Circus had arrived in trucks and set up east of town for their parade. The piping, raspy notes of the calliope reached our ears long before the wagons came into sight. Excitement grew with every note, and I remember how we all leaned forward and stretched up to catch the very first peek.

We stood on a grassy hillside because Thompson Falls (Montana) was pretty much all hill on the north side of Main Street and watched the magic unfold in front of us. It really was a *real* circus! Everyone said they couldn't believe a circus had come to our little town! Not only did they have beautifully painted wagons with smiling, waving circus people, but there were also lions in cages and even an elephant! I remember the elephant.

I recall little else of that day, except a nagging shadow of disappointment.

I had expected it to be the Barnum & Bailey Circus. You know, "The Greatest Show on Earth." I had childishly hoped that someone in the circus would have remembered my grandma and could have told us what happened to her. But no one in the Carson & Barnes Circus would have known my grandma, because she had been with Barnum & Bailey. It's funny that I remember that sadness.

The legend of "Circus Grandma:"

First, Circus Grandma was really my great-grandmother. She was my father's mother's mom. We didn't know her name.

She had been an acrobat, one that performed on the broad backs of those huge white show horses that trot rhythmically around the big sawdust ring of the circus.

Her ability to do tricks on horses was a natural talent, no doubt born of her Native American heritage. She had run away from the reservation as a young girl to join the circus. The colorblindness, so prevalent in the family, was summarily attributed to her Indian blood.

Nothing turns a story into bona fide legend like tragedy. While in London, England with the Barnum & Bailey Circus she fell from a horse and died, leaving her young daughter, Jenny, my dad's mother, an orphan.

Jeannette "Jenny" Riffle suffered a heart attack and passed away 23 May 1958, not quite making it to her seventy-second birthday. Her life story was simple. She was orphaned while a young girl when her circus mother died in London. Somehow, she ended up living in the Riffle household in Wisconsin. In 1904, at the age of eighteen while still living with the Riffle family but in North Dakota, she married the youngest son in the household, Charles Earnest "Ernie" Riffle.

My dad was the youngest of Jenny and Ernie's nine children. Ruby was the first being born in 1905. Earl, Hazel, Grace, George and Floyd (Bud) followed her, each of them breathing their first breath in Hettinger County, Rifle Township, North Dakota. The family name was often spelled "Rifle" back then. Rifle Township was likely named after the family. Anyway, the story was that the drought forced the family to abandon the homestead and move to Sandpoint, Idaho where Charles was born in 1919, and Raymond in 1922. In 1924 the family left Sandpoint for greener pastures in Norwich, New York. The Riffles had many "old roots" in that area to return to. There my father, Clarence "Cap" Riffle, was born in 1926.

The 1924 Rifle Migration ~ Idaho to New York.

They lived through the Depression, struggling in ways no one would ever talk about. We do know that Ernie eked out a living on a dairy farm. He walked several miles every day before catching a ride to the farm. When he returned in the evening, he would have a lunch pail full of butter and a loaf of bread under each arm. That was supper.

Jenny and Ernie lost their second-born son when he was a teenager in January of 1933. A kid had put lead nails in the moonshine jug as a joke. George drank from the jug and died of lead poisoning. Dad said they put a mirror in front of George's face so they could tell when he stopped breathing. He remembers sitting outside on the hospital steps because he was too young to be allowed inside. Although the family was dirt poor, Ernie hired professional "criers" to walk behind the casket in the funeral procession and "cry" for the deceased.

Somewhere around 1937, Jenny and her family migrated back to Sandpoint, Idaho by way of Tacoma, Washington, where daughter Ruby lived at the time. Ernie and Jenny did logging and odd jobs to make ends meet in Idaho. They were still poor. Charlie, their third youngest, was the second son to perish. He died in a freak accident at the mill in Colburn, Idaho in October of 1950. Charlie was electrocuted when a crane he was standing on, got tangled up in a power line.

My grandfather, his remaining seven children and their spouses, my brother and I, and our cousins attended my Grandmother Jenny's funeral services. We sat behind a curtain in the Moon Chapel funeral home, hidden from the public. When the sermon ended, we were invited to form a line and file past Jenny's open casket. I was grateful that I was too short to see inside; but to my horror, my mother lifted me up. I was not sad to see my dead grandmother. I was terrified. That night, my mother asked my brother and me to pray for Grandma

Jenny. To my lifelong shame, I did not. It had nothing to do with my affection for my grandmother. I was mad at my mom for lifting me up.

With the whole family gathered, they must have discussed Jenny's life and her "circus mother." We younger cousins were enchanted by this wonderful story. What a magnificent thing to have had a famous grandmother with the Barnum & Bailey Circus who had traveled to London. It did not matter one bit to us kids that she was already dead. She was part of a famous circus.

The fairytale legend of our circus grandmother smoldered like the roots of a burning tree. Marriages were made and broken; children were born, grew up, left the nest, and made their own families. Jenny's descendants all knew they were part Indian, and most were exceedingly proud of it.

While many of us looked for information on Circus Grandma, we always came up empty-handed. Jenny's maiden name had been "Jeannette Leona White." And since Jenny was proud of the fact that she got her middle name from her mother, we concluded that Jenny's mother's first name must have been "Leona" and her married surname, White.

Before census records were available online, a cousin found Jenny in the federal census of 1900 on microfiche. We discovered that Jenny had a brother, never before mentioned. The census, taken 22 June 1900, recorded that Jenny (fourteen, born July 1886) and her younger brother Charles (eleven, born February 1889) were born in Illinois, their father in New York, and their mother in Illinois. They were "boarders" at the Riffle farm in Lena, Wisconsin.

Sporadically we looked for Leona White in circus and library archives and on Internet genealogy sites, but we found nothing relevant. Jenny's father had been a "traveling salesman." No one had ever known his name, not even my grandmother. Where had he gone? Why didn't he take care of Jenny and her brother when their mother fell off that horse in England?

Fifty-four years after that funeral, we found Circus Grandma. Two cousins-in-law, one stranger, my son, and I—we found her. We couldn't believe it at first. The real story was more amazing than the legend. It's as if the moon and stars lined up and finally, we found her.

Like most things, rooting out the truth was just a matter of time and persistence.

Although we knew about Jenny's little brother (Charles) because of that 1900 census in Lena, Wisconsin, we had no other information about him. Luckily, by 1998 genealogy websites had sprung up across the Internet. Having some time to kill one day, I did a search on the Riffle name and low and behold, Charles's family was also looking for us, Jenny's family!

Charles Joseph White was Jenny's brother's full name. He had run away from the Riffle farm in North Dakota sometime after 1900. He died 24 October 1932. He was only forty-three years old. He had been out on a search and rescue mission in the mountains. A rock fell on him and crushed his head in Sawpit Canyon near Los Angeles. My own father was only six when his Uncle Charles died, so it is no wonder our family never knew about Jenny's little brother.

We cousins excitedly compared notes about Charles and Jenny's mother. Although these two branches of family had been separated for over sixty years, the legend of Circus Grandma matched almost perfectly, right down to the Indian reservation and white horses. Still, tangible evidence about her eluded us.

For years we held key information but did not recognize it. We had Jenny's 1958 death certificate and it listed Madilee Price as her mother. But since we were convinced her mother's name was Leona White, we ignored it, believing it had been written in error. Jenny's father was listed as "unknown."

Charles's descendants had searched for years in vain for a certificate of marriage for Charles White and his wife, Nora Jesme. They believed the marriage took place in North Dakota or South Dakota where Nora was born. It turns out their assumption was wrong. The long sought-after marriage record popped up on a simple Internet search in 2012. The couple had been married in Los Angeles County in 1918. And while most marriage records list only the names of the bride and groom, we got lucky, and the names of their parents were also listed. Charles's parents were listed as Mattie L. Price and William W. White.

Two official documents, one from a 1918 marriage license and one forty years later on a 1958 death certificate concurred, Madilee Price aka Mattie L. Price was the mother of Jenny and Charles White. Mattie Lee Price had to be the real name of our Circus Grandma.

The race was on! Fingers across several states, including Hawaii, pounded computer keyboards frantically seeking out this Mattie Lee Price on the Internet. Links leading to hints about her life were immediate and plentiful, but what we found was incredibly hard to believe. The family legend said, "acrobat," but historical records skirted around the idea of her being incredibly strong, maybe even magical.

We found a bounty of breadcrumbs, little tidbits of her life sprinkled liberally in various parts of the world. Her story tumbled out of history backward, sideways, and upside down. Mattie's public life was richly documented in domestic and foreign newspaper articles and advertisements, scientific publications, census records, legal documents, books, and online repositories. Recorded by journalists and sensationalized by advertisers, her life story grew nevertheless more clearly defined. Not only could we imagine who she was by what was written, we could discern a bit of her character by what was left unsaid.

Our research has led us to conclude that Mattie Lee Price was born near Rome, Georgia, on 19 May 1869, four years after the end of the Civil War. One can imagine that the shells of burned buildings had yet to fall and forests and fields still showed black from Sherman's 1864 March to the Sea.

Life was different back then when Mattie grew up. And while it is fun to read about performers in the circus of days gone by, it is also sobering to get a glimpse into the reality of their lives. We live in a time of exploding science and discovery, smartphones and radio-controlled drones, but in Mattie's youth almost everything was still a mystery. There were no airplanes, telephones, or flushing toilets on a simple farm in Georgia in the 1880s. We cannot pass judgment about what we found out about Mattie or her family. It was a different time with a whole different set of circumstances.

The Civil War affected Mattie's family and thus it affected her, which in turn affected her children and her children's children. One might think that history is about someone else, about a general or a president or some old guy in the rest home, but each American who has familial roots deep in this country has been affected by its past. Generation after generation, we pass along our experiences. Our family culture grows, bends, and survives. History matters because it is part of what made us what we are today.

Mattie Lee Price, the name our family never knew, and Georgia almost completely forgot, is threaded through a part of American history and culture that should be better remembered. Entertainment history during her public era between 1884 and 1899 has been primarily represented by miniscule mentions in books on circuses and dime museums. Most often the writers include only a sentence or two about this period as a sort of "transitional glue" between the early 1800s and the 1920s.

Mattie began in Georgia and so shall we.

The earliest record we found of Mattie was from 1880. She was just another little girl living on a farm with her family. She was listed as Mattie Price in the 1880 federal census in Georgia. She was marked as "twelve," but we know now that she had just turned eleven. She was born in Georgia and did not attend school.

Mattie's father was listed as George Price, thirty-four, born in Georgia. His thirty-two-year-old wife, Elizabeth Price, was born in North Carolina. There were three younger children: William, five; Georgia, three; and Francis, one.

George's parents (William E. and Alvira Price), his maternal grandparents (James and Henrietta Burks), as well as some of his siblings and cousins lived in households listed one after the other in adjacent households on the same page.

While many southerners lost everything in the Civil War, Mattie's paternal grandfather, William E. Price, managed to hold on to his land. His extended family likely needed one another to survive, and it is conceivable they were all living off the Price farmland in 1880.

The place itself was recorded as Bull Pen, 153rd Division, and is situated in the northeastern county of Murray, Georgia. It is beautiful land situated at the foot of the Cohutta Mountains, often referred to as "Spring Place." Located in the heart of the Cherokee Nation before the Indians were removed from 1838–1839, the land is drenched in Native American heartache and history. However, the Price farm was not on an Indian reservation, nor was a single name on the census page recorded as "Indian." With the exception of one black male, everyone on the page was counted "W" or white.

Obviously, if Mattie did not live on an Indian reservation, she could not have run away from one. So why then did her descendants all believe the Indian legend was true even without evidence? The answer could be in that old saying, "Looks can be deceiving." Jenny, Mattie's blue-eyed daughter, had nine children. While several were lean, blond, and blue eyed, a few had coarse black hair, brown eyes, and a short stocky build. Naturally the dark ones were attributed to the legendary Indian heritage. Female colorblindness is extraordinarily rare, but Jenny was indeed colorblind. We know that her sons and grandsons inherited this condition from her. Since this came from Jenny, it was believed to be another Indian trait. Lastly, but the least comfortable to recall, was the alcoholism. A few of Jenny's sons "drank too much," and that trait was also (unfairly) attributed to that Indian blood.

Since we found no evidence of Native American heritage, we did DNA testing on both Jenny's granddaughter and her brother, Charles's grandson. This revealed absolutely no Native American blood, not a drop, hint, or trace. Four generations had believed wholeheartedly in a Native American Indian legend that was untrue!

Shock reverberated through the whole family as the news spread; there was no Indian heritage. Family nonagenarians and octogenarians alike stood their ground, refusing to believe that the "legend" they had perpetuated for up to seventy years was a lie.

If Mattie Lee Price wasn't Indian and hadn't run away from a reservation, what *was* her story? We dug a little deeper and soon realized that the woman listed in the 1880 census as George Price's wife was not Mattie's biological mother. There was more to the story.

It seems that George Washington Price and Rhoda P. McAbee, both native Georgians, were married in Floyd County, Georgia 22

April 1868. Mattie showed up about eleven months later. ("Georgia, County Marriages, 1785–1950," index and images, FamilySearch https://familysearch.org/pal:/MM9.1.1/KXJ5-GKB: accessed 30 January 2015; George W. Price and Rhoda McAbee, 03 May 1868; citing marriage, Floyd, Georgia, United States, county courthouses, Georgia; FHL microfilm 282,712).

Two more children followed Mattie, a boy and a girl. (We do not know their names). Rhoda's widowed father, Lacy McAbee, and some of Rhoda's siblings migrated to a place near Richwoods, Arkansas sometime after they were counted in the 1870 federal census, in Chattooga, Georgia. Apparently, George, Rhoda, and the three children decided to follow the McAbee migration west.

Something went terribly wrong in Arkansas. Rhoda and her two youngest children perished. George Price was left alone with Mattie, who must have been about four. Rebecca Elizabeth Penland (according to the Civil War pension records she filed in 1929) married the widowed George Price in Independence, Arkansas on 18 January 1874. (Texas State Library and Archives Commission; Austin, Texas; Confederate Pension Applications, 1899-1975; Collection #: CPA16526; Roll #: 2631; Roll Description: Pension File Nos. 00023 to 63977, Application Years 1899 to 1935).

Mattie's new stepmother and George Price had their first son, William Edward Franklin Price, in October of 1874 while still living in Arkansas. We assume they moved back to the Price family farm in Murray County, Georgia before their daughter, Georgia Alvira Price was born in 1877. After all, who names a girl Georgia while they're still living in Arkansas?

At some point after the 1880 federal census and prior to the summer of 1883, George Price moved his family about sixty miles south to a place near Cartersville, Georgia. Records show that George rented a farm from landowner, J. W. Williams. The farm was on the

Euharlee River and lay a couple of miles northwest of Stilesboro, a small community outside of Cartersville.

The summer of 1883 had been terribly hot and the land produced skimpy crops. Farmers, especially those renting farms, had a difficult time making ends meet. By Christmas of that year, George Price would have had a lot on his plate. He had a heavily pregnant wife, a daughter (Mattie, fourteen) from his first marriage, and four small children (aged nine, six, five, and one) to provide for. Ella had joined siblings William, Georgia and Francis in June 1882. January of 1884 brought miserably cold weather to the south and a brand-new baby girl, Emma.

There can be little doubt that Mattie was a vital pair of helping hands on the Price farm. Her list of chores would have been endless, even in winter when there was no cotton to pick. Casual trips into town to socialize would have been out of the question; but make no mistake, Mattie would have been well informed about local goings-on. People on farms kept up on all the latest news. Gossip, after all, is a farm dweller's best entertainment.

Folks in rural settings generally know the longest held secrets of their neighbors. Prejudices for or against another local can survive several generations. Locals know what folks are getting married, getting born, getting old, or getting buried. They know who got a new horse, a new hog, or a new buggy. If someone got a raw deal from a tradesman, everybody knew it. There just aren't many secrets in country living.

The most spectacular gossipy topic in the winter of 1883–1884 was Lula Hurst from nearby Polk County. Either folks had seen her themselves or they knew someone who had. Mattie would have been just as excited as everyone else to hear news of Lula. It was juicy news and much more exciting than anything like twin calves that might have been born to a neighbor's cow down the road.

# — Chapter Two —

*L*ULA HURST WAS THE TALK of Georgia by late 1883. She lived near Cedartown, about seventeen miles from the Price farm. Although she was only a youthful fifteen-year-old child, she had already baffled large audiences with her inexplicable feats of strength.

Maybe it was the boring winter weather that inspired her to invent a set of tricks to entertain her friends and family, tricks that somehow went public. Who knows? She will never tell. Regardless of what actually inspired the invention of her so-called magical powers, the mystery set the imaginations of Georgians on fire! One can suppose that once she got a lot of attention through newspaper accounts, personal interviews, doctor examinations, and demands for demonstrations for which she was handsomely paid, it became impossible for her to simply confess to how the tricks worked and walk away from the whole business. Lula and her family invented an entire backstory to explain how "the power" first manifested itself and how that power used Lula's feminine hands to do seemingly impossible things.

In her autobiography, *Lulu Hurst (The Georgia Wonder) Writes Her Autobiography, and For the First Time Explains and Demonstrates the Great Secret of Her Marvelous Power*, Lula tells the tale of how the mystical power manifested itself one stormy night on the family farm near Cedartown. Never in her lifetime did she admit that it was all a hoax. Newspapers often reported that Lula "giggled" during her demonstrations. She must have laughed all the way to the bank.

Newspapers of that day and age printed a lot of unsubstantiated stories. Whatever crazy gossip surfaced was printed in the local rag. The more bizarre the story, the more attention was given. The *Athens Banner Weekly*, based in Athens, Georgia, gave Lula's 29 December 1883 demonstration in Rome, Georgia, the front page, center column spot. Incredibly, the editor dedicated almost the entire column to Lula. And, to substantiate Lula's story, the reporter wrote that her cousin was with her when manifestations of power moved a bed mysteriously by itself and a series of strange thumping noises emanated from her bed's headboard. Miss Wimberly claimed to have felt a "shock" from the "power" in the bedroom where the girls were staying. Perhaps this reported shock is why the press began to dub the Georgia girl, "electric" as well as magnetic. (*Athens Weekly Banner*, Tuesday 8 January 1884. P.1, Col 5).

On that same front page was another bizarre article titled, "A Strange Phenomenon." An ill, wealthy farmer complained about rocks falling from the ceiling. Some were warm, some were wet, and none of them left a hole in the ceiling. Members of the family believed that the rocks might have been a warning of the farmer's impending death. Strange stories sold newspapers, so they were printed, rational or not.

Publications called Lula's strength "supernatural" and wonderful and inexplicable that winter of 1883–1884. Some wrote that she had acquired the gift of magnetism and they sometimes called her "the Georgia Magnetic Girl." With all of that attention and money to be made, one can imagine that lots of people attempted to duplicate what Lula Hurst did. Indeed, many men were able to replicate Lula's feats of strength, but they were men and not fifteen-year-old girls, so their proof was instantly set aside.

Lula appeared in opera houses and other public venues, always accompanied by her mother and father. She was, after all, a gentle southern maiden from a good family—people to be believed and trusted.

Lula's father, Mr. W. E. Hurst, who had been an officer in the Confederate army, hailed from Tennessee. He'd relocated to Georgia sometime after his hometown was destroyed in the War Between the States. He was a respected man in Polk County, Georgia, and a deacon in the Baptist church. Lula's mother was the daughter of a Baptist preacher. Lula's uncle (her mother's brother), Rev. Jesse Wood, was a well-known Baptist preacher and the president of Woodland Female College in Cedar Valley. Lula's mother had homeschooled her on the farm until she was about eleven years old. Then the family moved into Cedartown in order to further Lula's education.

After Lula's so called "powers" became public in 1883, Lula and her family always claimed publicly that Lula was born in Georgia in 1869. A younger "Georgia Wonder" was more marketable. However, in the 1870 census, which was recorded on August 20, she was listed as two years old and native to Tennessee. In 1880, the census noted that she was eleven years old and born in Tennessee; but this was recorded on 1 June. From this we gather that she was born between

1 June and 20 August of 1868 in Tennessee. Indeed, the 1900 federal census, where she appears as Lula Atkinson wife of Paul Atkinson, it is recorded that she was born in Tennessee in June. It might be fairly safe to assume that her accurate birthdate was June of 1868. However, Lula's tombstone has her dubious birth year carved indelibly in stone, "1869–1950." Of course, it doesn't matter at all that she (perhaps) fibbed about her rightful age; she was a southern belle. Keeping one's age a secret was allowed and probably outright expected.

By mid-January 1884, Lula Hurst was going great guns, raking in the money, and demonstrating her amazing abilities in front of large audiences several times a week. Even in the very beginning, her profit for a single evening could easily reach $100, a handsome sum in the 1880s. The excitement over Lula increased exponentially as taletellers retold and exaggerated stories.

What a welcome diversion it must have been for a farm girl like Mattie to take the wagon into town, especially in that cold winter of 1883–1884. She would be able to see other people, gossip, and maybe sell a few eggs to the grocer. Just imagine how exciting it must have been for her to witness the most wonderful thing that had happened to Georgia in years: Miss Lula Hurst!

Mattie Lee Price saw Lula Hurst sometime in January of 1884.

The timetable and how Mattie could have seen Lula Hurst are a little hazy. Newspaper articles were often undated and frequently appeared in weekly newspapers rather than daily ones. A piece about Lula could have been written on one Friday for the next Friday's paper about an appearance that took place on the previous Friday! Thus, an account could be two weeks old before it ever went to press!

Lula wrote in her autobiography that she discovered her powers in September of 1883, however the first account of Lula's demonstrations did not surface until late December that year. Apparently, the public had been invited to visit the Hurst farm five miles outside of Cedartown to observe the girl in person.

The Cedartown Advertiser submitted an article to the *Atlanta Weekly Constitution* on 1 January 1884 stating that the Cedartown reporter had gone to witness Lula's magic himself, "on Thursday evening past." That would have been 27 December 1883. (Georgia by Wire. Specials to the Constitution. Cedartown December 27, the *Atlanta Constitution*, Sat 29 Dec 1883 p. 2, col. 3).

Lula's first stage presentation was scheduled for 31 December 1883 in nearby Cedartown. That event was postponed until the "last of next week" or the fourth of January 1884. (The *Atlanta Constitution*, Sun 30 Dec 1883, p. 3, col. 6).

As Atlanta was being pelted with four inches of fresh snow on 12 January 1884, Lula was making a name for herself in Floyd County, Rome, Georgia. The *Atlanta Constitution* reported that she would perform again in Rome on the fourteenth. (15 Jan 1884, p. 2, col. 2) It was fifteen degrees below in Rome on the fifteenth, according to the *Athens Weekly Banner* (15 Jan 1884, p. 1, col. 3). In spite of the cold, Lula was still bending sticks and lifting men in chairs in Rome on the sixteenth. Audiences were amazed. (The *Atlanta Constitution*, 17 Jan 1884, p. 7, col. 2).

A reporter for the *Weekly Constitution* (Atlanta) wrote, "Had a private séance" at Lula's hotel in Rome, Georgia, around the fifteenth. Lula's parents were there as well. From the beginning, the press loved Lula Hurst.

"Freeman, of the *Cedartown Advertiser*, and Ponder, of the *Rome Courier*, have both staked their sacred honor on Lula Hurst's beauty," read the article in the *Chicago Tribune* by 20 January. Lula was said to be "15 years old, unusually large for her age, and her wrists are as big as those of a good-sized man."

The *Cartersville American* reported on the twenty-second that Lula was in Rockmart, Georgia, "last week." The event would have taken place between the sixteenth and the twenty-first of January 1884. (The *Cartersville American*, 22 Jan 1884). Rockmart is about ten miles south of the Price farm. It is unlikely that Mattie would have driven the distance to see Lula even if she was Georgia's biggest sensation. It is more likely that Lula Hurst and her parents got off the train at every whistle stop and gave an exhibition. And there is a very high probability that one of those whistle stops was at the Stilesboro Academy. Could it have been purely accidental that Mattie just happened to be nearby when Lula got off that train sometime between the sixteenth and twenty-first of January 1884?

Inspired and excited after witnessing the wonderful Lula Hurst, Mattie probably went straight home and demonstrated the act for her little brother and sisters. She could never have imagined that her ability to easily replicate Lula's feats would almost immediately propel her to the stage as the Second Georgia Wonder.

By the twenty-ninth of January 1884, the *Cartersville American*, Mr. Wilkes, proprietor, reported that Lula Hurst might already have a rival. "Mr. G. W. Price an unpretending citizen of this community claims that his daughter possesses a power similar and as wonderful as that of Miss Lula Hurst, and a demonstration of which will be attempted at the academy next Wednesday night." The academy mentioned was, of course, the Stilesboro Academy, about eight miles southwest of Cartersville and readily accessible by horse or rail.

The sensational news spread quickly. Just three days later, the *Atlanta Constitution* ran an article referencing both Lula and Mattie under "Georgia Gossip." "Magnetic girls are now the rage in Georgia. Miss Hurst, after scoring great success in Atlanta, went to Chattanooga where she failed to materialize to suite the people. As soon as she appeared before a Georgia audience, however, in Cartersville, chairs flew around in wild confusion and wonder stood in awe." The piece openly made fun of the magnetic-girl craziness and reported that a girl in Dawson "could sit down on a hollow log and attract everything toward her within a distance of sixty feet." The joyful commentary concluded with, "Mr. G. W. Price an unpretending citizen of this community claims that his daughter possesses a power similar and as wonderful as that of Miss Lula Hurst, and a demonstration of which will be attempted at the academy next Wednesday night." (The *Atlanta Constitution*, 1 Feb 1884, p. 2, col. 1).

On 5 February 1884, the *Atlanta Constitution* reported under Cartersville news, "Both Miss Hurst and Miss Price came up on the Cedartown train. Miss Hurst will entertain the people of Marietta tonight." It was remarkable how Mattie, a fourteen-year-old farm girl with virtually no social standing, became so quickly mentioned in such an important newspaper.

"A Peculiar Stock Company," was the title of a 5 February 1884 article involving Mattie in the *Weekly Cartersville American*. The investors in this stock company were none other than three of the most important gentlemen in Cartersville: Mr. Patillo, Col. A. P. Wofford, and Mr. Dock Cunyus. They planned to give Mattie a little training, a wardrobe, and a manager and then show her off around the South, hoping for a tidy return on their investment. (Note that the name Cunyus was often confused with Conyers and both names were frequently misspelled in newspaper accounts).

A Peculiar Stock Company.

Talk about Cartersville being a slow town, or pokey, or behind the times! It's all stuff and nonsense. You can't find a more progressive town in Georgia. The latest thing out, and the only thing of the kind out, is a stock company to exhibit the Bartow county WONDER,—Miss Mattie Lee Price. The company is composed of Mr. Robert M. Patillo, Col. A. P. Wofford and Mr. Dock Cunyus—All Bartow county men,— They propose to put Miss Price under a short training in order to fully test and develop her powers. An elegant wardrobe will be prepared, and in a week or two she will be ready for the road. The first exhibition will be given at Cartersville, and if it proves satisfactory they will at once map out a tour and take in all the southern cities. Mr. Patillo is very sanguine and has given her peculiar powers a sufficient test to satisfy his skeptical mind. Dock Cunyurs will make a mashing stage manager, and don't you forget it. Success to the new enterprise, Hope they will all get very rich and divide the profits with the printers.—Hurrah for Bartow county! still ahead!

Courtesy of the Bartow History Museum, Cartersville, Georgia

A second article in the same weekly newspaper told the story of Mattie's premier performance. The account of the show was long and descriptive. The paper's editor appeared to have been a friend to the investors and thus favorably biased. "Stilesboro Siftings" was the title of the article that was signed simply "subscriber."

Miss Mattie Lee Price a daughter of Mr. G.W. Price a poor unpretentious citizen who resides about one and a half miles from this place was hand-billed last week to exhibit a mysterious Electrical Power which she claimed to possess at the academy on Wednesday night. Upon the whole thing was a humbug, but we went up simply to gratify curiosity. On arriving at the academy we found a small audience who had come to see this second Lula Hurst. When Miss Price went upon the stage, we judged her to be about 14 years old and weighing about ninety pounds. She is rather slender, with dark complexion, blue eyes, and brown hair. She was plainly but neatly dressed.

She began the performance by placing her hands upon the back of a chair, in which sat the portly local editor of the Free Press, but his avoirdupois was too much for her electrical powers, and the chair didn't move worth a cent; but, when he caught it in his arms, she skipped him around with perfect ease. Then Tom Culpepper sat in the chair. Tom weighs two hundred, and is the best man in the community. Presently he made three "back" jumps across the stage and brought up on the floor. Mr. Joel Conyers then sat on his lap, but they were hurled to the floor with all ease. We then went upon the stage and caught hold of a large stick, and Miss Price placed one hand gently on the one end, and we began to slip and slide about the stage. Uncle Peter Hammond then went to the stage declaring that he was stout. He caught hold of the stick, and Miss Mattie placed her hands against each end of the stick, and he began to "swing corners and promenade." While Miss Price certainly does possess some mysterious power, yet all this was augmented by her physical strength, which she undoubtedly exerted.

Telegraph wires in Georgia lit up with the news that Lula Hurst had a real rival in Mattie Lee Price. In the 12 February 1884 edition of the *Athens Banner-Watchman* there was a center column, front-page article. The story of Mattie's first performance had been reprinted from the *Cartersville Free Press*. The headline read, "Mattie Lee Price. Bartow County Possess a Wonderful Electro-Magnetic Girl." According to the lengthy, but not completely accurate, account of Mattie's first performance as an "Electro-Magnetic Girl" the demonstrations were successfully executed at Stilesboro Academy.

The Stilesboro Academy where both Mattie and Lula exhibited still stands. It is an old wooden building that was built in 1859 to serve as a school for the local community.

Stilesboro Academy

Stilesboro Academy interior

The wooden structure has one huge center room called the chapel and two very large classrooms, one on either side of the chapel. Each classroom has its own entrance. Fourteen-foot-high double entry doors lead into the chapel, which boasts twenty-foot ceilings. Three impressive windows on the far end of the room mirror the height of the entry doors. A hand-painted banner arches over the center window and stretches out over to touch the top of the outer two windows. The foot tall letters proclaim, "*Deo Ac Patriac.*" Legend has it that this motto (To God and Country) was the reason General Sherman did not torch the building.

The aforementioned *Athens Banner-Watchman* article insinuated that Mattie had more power than Lula, and this was especially important given that Mattie was younger, smaller, and less experienced. The reporter further validated the integrity of Mattie's talent by listing the names of some of Carterville's most important men, all of whom believed she was the real deal. Peter Hammond, Van B. McGinnis, and Joel Conyers "and scores of others."

On the second page of the same paper was a little magnetic gossip. Under "Telegraphic Sparks" the reporter wrote that Lula's father had called Mattie a fraud. "Mr. Hurst seems inclined to create a corner on the humbug business," added the correspondent. "Don't be too greedy."

On the third page, they reported that Mattie had "exhibited in Cartersville Monday night, at the residence of Mayor Wofford and in the presence of a few showed her wonderful 'electrical powers.' Immediately after the performance her services were engaged for this year at $10,000."

So, although the newspaper stories published somewhat out of sequence, it seems obvious that Mattie observed Lula, auditioned for the town's important men the next Monday, and then gave her first performance the following Wednesday. The stock company wasted no time getting their little moneymaker on stage.

# — Chapter Three —

*M*ATTIE LEE PRICE AND LULA Hurst were fortunate in that their acts emerged during a particularly sweet spot in time. One of the conditions that contributed to their popularity was an increase in personal leisure time. Rural populations were migrating to cities in great numbers to take their place in the Industrial Revolution. While one rarely runs out of things to do on a farm, the rapidly increasing numbers of city dwellers were often given Sundays off to spend with their families.

Had the girls arrived on scene a few years earlier when the country was busy rebuilding after the Civil War, "John Q. Public" would have had little time or money to be interested in them. Any later, and that same public would have come to understand the basic scientific principles behind their muscular demonstrations. Such knowledge would have rendered the Georgia magnetic girl act a boring waste of time.

Academic science was burgeoning in 1884. Scientific magazines carefully collected information and it was being shared as never before. The public had become earnestly engaged in learning everything they could about the world around them, especially with regard to electricity, magnetism, and the world of the occult.

Newspapers fueled public curiosity about the emerging sciences. Unsubstantiated tales of miracle cures were printed in abundance. As previously mentioned, a report did not have to be true to be included in a newspaper. The fact that a story sparked public interest and therefore sold more newspapers was enough to warrant inclusion.

In column six of the 1 February 1884 *Atlanta Constitution* there was an enormous advertisement in which Dr. T. B. Little promised a miracle cure for cancer. "No Cure, No Pay!" And, although advertisers promised, with absolute certainty, cures for typhoid, cholera, and consumption, Teddy Roosevelt who was working in the New York legislature at the time, lost both his mother (typhoid fever) and wife (Bright's disease) on Valentine's Day that year. His daughter, Alice, was just two days old.

There were abundant newspaper drawings and diagrams advertising the medicinal use of magnetism and electricity. Magnetic clothing was advertised for sale, promising cures for just about everything from sore eyes to impotence. Magnetism was fascinating, not at all understood, and frequently confused with the term "animal magnetism."

Neither was electricity common to the everyday lives of Georgians in 1884. Atlanta had only just begun to electrify its streetlights. The general population had little understanding of how it worked.

There were also those advertisers claiming a spiritual connection to the world of the dead. The *Atlanta Constitution* openly advertised séances with mediums daily.

Lula Hurst showed up right in the middle of this scientific revolution and excited the minds of scientists as well as everyday people. Surely it must have been one of the three, magnetism, electricity, or spiritualism that allowed her to lift three men in a chair! She was Georgia's premier electro-magnetic girl. And while Lula never admitted to a spiritual element to her strength, everyone believed there was one.

Doctors poked, prodded, tested, and took her pulse and temperature, trying to discover the science behind her uncanny strength.

While Lula was riding a highly publicized wave of popularity and demonstrating her talents for large audiences filled with professors, medical doctors, and politicians, Mattie Lee Price set out somewhat more quietly on her own magnetic tour.

Lula was fortunate in that she had her mother, father, and Mr. Paul Atkinson her manager and future husband with her to support her and fend off any negative reactions to her shows. Mattie, on the other hand, was left in the company of her father and one or more male members of the stock company. No woman was ever mentioned as accompanying her as a chaperone.

The *Cartersville American* alluded to trouble with the stock company early on when on 19 February 1884, it printed, "Ask Dock Cunyus what he thinks of Mattie Lee Price. (Somebody will yet live to regret that they asked Dock Cunyus that question.—Ed)" Then, under "Stilesboro Siftings" on 4 March, the wind blew in the opposite direction when an anonymous "subscriber" reported, "Private letters received here state that the Mattie Lee Price combination is meeting with grand success."

On 9 April 1884, the *Huntsville Weekly Democrat* (Alabama) reported that Mattie "exhibited her marvelous strength at the Opera House last Monday night." Mr. Thos. W. White, Mr. R. E. Murphy, and Capt. Jas. E. Daniel stacked themselves, one atop the other, onto a "common split bottom chair" and tried to hold it down. But even with their combined weight of over 600 pounds, Mattie lifted the chair. Later Ernest Robinson, Esq. "held a green hickory stick between his knees and with his hands and Mr. C.H. Halsey united in holding the stick, and she laid the palm of her right hand on the top of the stick, which was, at least, an inch in diameter, and twisted it around…"

According to the *Cartersville American*, on 22 April 1884, Mattie was home "resting for another tour." She could not have rested much though, because on the twenty-ninth, the same publication reported that she had given an exhibition on the twenty-second at the Stiles-boro Academy. The writer indicated that no "wonders" had been reported, so it probably hadn't gone well. Mr. Joel Conyers was to be Mattie's "advance agent." On the twenty-eighth and twenty-ninth of April, Mattie exhibited at Adairsville, about twenty miles north of Cartersville.

She was in Kingston, Georgia, about twenty miles northwest of Cartersville on 1 May 1884. An article in the *Cartersville American* on the sixth, submitted by a Kingston reporter, shines a very favorable light on Mattie's skills. Several gentlemen at Cobb's Hall in Kingston had witnessed her strength and lent their names to endorse her publicly as being "no humbug."

## MISS MATTIE LEE PRICE AT KINGSTON.

### Miraculous Feats.

TO THE PUBLIC:—We, the undersigned, citizens of Kingston, Ga., and vicinity, hereby certify that we witnessed one of Miss Mattie Lee Price's performances, at Cobb's Hall, at this place, on the night of May the 1st. We conscientiously and cheerfully endorse Miss Price as a success. She certainly possesses some wonderful power which is absolutely irresistible. We saw, with our own eyes, that she raised (by simply placing the palms of her hands on the posts of a chair) the weight of a chair, with that of four large men upon it—over seven hundred pounds of actual weight. There were other evidences of her power, which to tell, would be a story incredible, but, nevertheless, true. Miss Price is no humbug, but is all, and even more, than she is represented to be.

Courtesy of the Bartow History Museum, Cartersville, Georgia

A *Dalton Citizen* newspaper article, which was subsequently reprinted in the *Athens Banner-Watchman* on 13 May 1884, announced that "Lula Hurst, No. 2" had "exhibited her wonderful powers at Trevitt hall…" on 6 May 1884. "What this mysterious power is we are unable to say; but that it is truly wonderful and without deception there can be no doubt." Mr. Conyers, Mattie's advance agent, was off in Kentucky, lining up a show at Clemens House in Stanford. Mattie showed in Huntsville first and then at the McDonald's Opera House in Montgomery around 10 May before moving on to Kentucky.

On 24 May 1884, she gave an exhibition at the opera house in Stanford, Kentucky. The *Semi Weekly Interior Journal* reported that her father and two neighbors named Conyers had accompanied Mattie. The troupe made no claim of "spiritualism," and Mattie never claimed to understand what the power was.

On 27 May 1884, Mattie appeared at the opera house in Frankfort, Kentucky. According to the *Frankfort Roundabout* on the thirty-first, she was "certainly a wonder." Her power could not be simply muscular, for "a good healthy gust of wind would blow her away."

Then on 25 May 1884 in the *Louisville Courier* in Kentucky, she was advertised as "Mattie Lee Price the Great Electro-Magnetic Girl" and she would be at the "Masonic Temple Theatre on Friday and Saturday Evenings and Saturday matinee, May 30 and 31. Admission 50 cents." Reserve tickets could be had at Rosenham & Co.'s drug store on the corner of Forth and Jefferson. Under "Amusement Notes" on the twenty-seventh, the *Louisville Courier* printed this endorsement:

> Prof. W. W. Legare, President of the Marion College; Dr. Whitehead, of Washington, D.C.; ex-Gov. Smith and several other prominent Alabama physicians have published the following certificate in reference to Miss Price: We take pleasure in stating that we have witnessed some of the feats performed my Miss Mattie Lee Price, and she gives satisfactory evidence of possessing some wonderful powers that we have not seen explained. Her exhibitions are above suspicion, and are worthy of scientific research. (The *Louisville Courier*, 27 May 1884; p. 6; col. 2).

This Masonic Temple performance was also written about in the *New York Dramatic Mirror*. The audience, the reporter wrote, was small because patrons were suspicious of a "snap and sell." Mattie was described as a simple country girl, awkward and modest, but "possessed of a power or influence (call it what you may) that knocks the sciences of natural physics and specific gravity into a cocked hat and drives the learned philosopher wild." The reporter continued with, "Here is a chance for some intelligent, enterprising New York manager and your correspondent will insure the venture."

The Louisville demonstration was also written about in the *Shelbyville Daily Democrat*, Shelbyville, Kentucky, on 2 June 1884. The description of Mattie was anything but flattering: "A dowdy-looking tangled-haired, blue-eyed country girl, weighing about ninety pounds, stood this afternoon in the center of a group of leading Louisville physicians and press representatives." George Price introduced his daughter and invited the audience to test her powers. The reporter wrote that she was "devoid of cultivation," and although called electric, no electricity was involved. After an hour, the doctors "pronounced her wonderful, and frankly admitted their inability to say what the power consisted, but it was certainly in her." Mattie was slated to appear in Shelbyville and in Cincinnati, Ohio.

The Mattie Lee Price Stock Company seemed off to a good start. Newspaper reports were mostly positive and medical men were mostly puzzled.

# — Chapter Four —

*C*INCINNATI GOT OFF ON THE wrong foot. The *Cincinnati Enquirer* had run a large advertisement for the Harris Mammoth Museum on 1 June, a Sunday. It proclaimed, "EXTRAORDINARY ENGAGEMENT at a salary of $1,000 per week, the Far-Famed GEORGIA ELECTRO-MAGNETIC GIRL Mattie Lee Price," would be there that very day. But Mattie's troupe arrived too late on 1 June 1884 to exhibit at Harris's Museum. Instead, a private "séance" was organized in one of the parlors of the Gibson House where doctors and members of the press were hastily invited. "Dr. Muscroft, Sr., Dr. P. S. Conner, Dr. Smuck, Dr. Heighway, Dr. Armstrong, Dr. Kirby, and others concurred in the opinion that she is one of the wonders of the age." On 2 June 1884, the *Cincinnati Tribune* reported that Mattie would finally be showing at Mr. Harris's Museum that day.

The *Atlanta Constitution*, 5 June 1884, reprinted a *Cincinnati Enquirer* article about the séance given on 1 June 1884 at the Gibson House. "The curious spectacle of a strong man holding a chair in his embrace with a death grip, and vainly trying to maintain a position on his feet against the power of a slightly-built girl of fourteen years, was witnessed last night in one of the Gibson House parlors." Dr. Muscroft Sr. called her power "dynamo-anonyma, or force without name." The doctors noted that although the gentlemen attempting to resist her power were sweating, the girl's pulse did not accelerate, and her temperature did not rise. One newspaper article estimated that over ten thousand people witnessed Mattie's skill set during her week at Harris's Mammoth Museum.

On 7 June 1884, an advertisement for the Harris Mammoth Museum ran in the *Sporting Theatrical* of Cincinnati, Ohio. Mattie Lee Price was slated to be there as well as Prof. John Hughs and his educated birds and three colorless children. On 8 June, there was to be one last exhibit of Mattie Lee Price, the "so-called Georgia electro-magnetic girl"; however, Mattie was not at the Harris Mammoth Museum as advertised. Instead, she was successfully astonishing the elite attendees of her show in Louisville, Kentucky on the night of the seventh. Among those she delighted and puzzled were "Governor Knott, Attorney General Hardin, Auditor Hewitt, Col. John R. Procter, Major Henry T. Stanton, the Hon. Ira Julian, Col. H. M. McCarty, Col. C. E. Bowman, General Daniel Lindsey, Dr. J.Q.A. Stewart, Dr. Sawyer, Dr. James, Dr. Hume, and Capt. Samuel M. Gaines."

The ninth of June 1884 was when things went seriously awry for Mattie's little stock company. Mr. Harris had requested that Mattie's manager prolong her engagement, which was impossible because they already had a contract with "Messers Anderson and & Miles" to entertain in Louisville and they could not break the engagement to entertain the governor of Kentucky! So, when Mattie went on stage in Louisville instead of Cincinnati on 7 June, Mr. Harris filed a lawsuit in the Common Pleas Court of Hamilton County, Ohio. *Harris v. Cumyns* was the name of the lawsuit in which Mr. Harris claimed that Mattie's managers deceived him. It was Dock Cunyus who was a member of the stock company, and we believe the name Cumyns is a misspelling of that name.

On 9 June, the *Cincinnati Commercial Gazette* published a lengthy article titled, "Only a Trick," in which the reporter gave some semblance of journalistic prudence to the dispute. This was touted as a "new and peculiar style of litigation" for the Common Pleas courts.

In the report, Mr. Harris stated that he had believed the agent had contracted the original electro-magnetic girl, Lula Hurst, to appear at the Harris Mammoth Museum for $100 per week and not Mattie Lee Price, an inexperienced young girl. Mr. Harris claimed that Mattie was neither electric nor magnetic but used pure muscular strength to lift chairs and bend sticks. He wanted $1,000 in damages. The same highly esteemed doctors who had witnessed Mattie at Gibson House and said the power was unexplainable were quick to shift their opinions and declare the act one of simple muscular power and leverage. "The girl may not be an intentional fraud," stated one of the pompous doctors.

Since Lula Hurst had been widely advertised, it is doubtful that Mr. Harris was fooled into believing that Mattie Lee Price was Lula Hurst. Also, his advertising on 1 June clearly stated that he had retained "Mattie Lee Price" at "$1,000 per week." If there was deception, perhaps both parties were complicit.

On the following day, the tenth, the *Cincinnati Enquirer* had its own lengthy report on the controversy. A couple of the witnesses at the Gibson House insisted that Mattie could not have done the feats on her own and there must be some other explanation. Others said she was just clever and it was leverage and fulcrum physics that provided the power, not some electrical or magnetic thing.

The *Enquirer* report read, in part:

The brothers Cunyus called at this office last night with a request for public notice that they were going to sue Manager Harris for $30,000 on account of financial injury done them and Mattie Lee Price, their electro-magnetic girl, in stating that she was a fraud. The gentleman through an accompanying friend, a Colonel from Georgia, said they were owners of plantations in the South, possessing of means amply sufficient to keep them without any occupation, and that they did not propose to be bulldozed by Mr. Harris. If necessary, they would stay here two years to fight this thing out.

In spite of the hullabaloo, Mattie travelled back to Cincinnati and gave a private exhibition at the Hotel Emory that very night, the tenth of June. Things did not go well. She couldn't lift men in chairs and the hickory stick didn't twist. "Mr. Cunyns, her manager, explained that she was not feeling well and might work to better advantage some other evening."

No mention of Mattie's father, George W. Price, was made in the newspapers after Mattie's first Cincinnati exhibition at the Gibson House on 1 July. Certainly he would not have known how to handle the whole lawsuit business; he was an uneducated farmer. Perhaps he simply hid away from the prying eyes of the press and, hopefully, shielded his daughter.

Mattie had just turned fifteen about two weeks before the Harris lawsuit was filed against her arrogant but inexperienced troupe. Newspaper reporters, medical men, and scientists had called her miraculous and then fraudulent—all in the same week. It must have been dizzying to be the center of so much attention and to bear the positive and negative scrutiny of so many strangers. She probably thought everything was her fault.

By July, the situation was clear: Mattie's little stock company had jumped the proverbial ship and hightailed it back to Georgia. "R.E.J. Miles made a contract with Cunyers of some remote portion of Georgia for the services of Miss Mattie Lee Price, the second of the wonders who is to lift chairs and break sticks," reported the *Buffalo Daily Courier* (20 July 1884; p. 2; col. 2). Mr. Miles, a very influential theater manager in Cincinnati, promptly countersued Mr. Harris of Cincinnati for $10,000 for defamation of Mattie's character (The *Evening Observer* (Dunkirk, New York), 23 June 1884, p. 3, col. 3). There was no further headline news about the lawsuit, but it was written up in the *Weekly Law Bulletin* of Columbus and Cincinnati, Ohio, that sixteenth day of June 1884. (Later this lawsuit was often referred to as one of the first to be filed with regard to an entertainer failing to deliver what was promised).

Even as Harris publicly proclaimed that magnetic girls were all humbug, he hypocritically got himself a brand new one—immediately. He announced that he'd taught "Little Flora," of Pittsburgh how to do Mattie's act and had set Flora upon his stage by 23 June. Magnetic girls were, after all, golden for bringing in large audiences.

The Mattie Lee Price Stock Company investors returned to Georgia unheralded. The *Cartersville American* editor, so quick to promote the wild adventure, printed not a single word about its miserable failure. The wealthy, plantation-owning investors were allowed to regain their dignity via silent press. As far as we know, Mattie's name was never again published in that town.

Mr. R.E.J. Miles wasted no time getting Mattie's name in print. In late June or early July of 1884, a silly, unsigned article appeared. The piece, which does not mention Mattie by name, was reprinted widely in various newspapers from as far west as North Dakota and Idaho to New York City between 1884 and 1886. Not having found the original publication, one can only surmise that Mr. Miles produced the piece right after he took over Mattie's contract.

"A Magnetic Girl," is set on a southbound train heading for Cincinnati. A "nice looking girl" was on the train when a young man, a drummer, stepped into the same car. The girl had bangs and lovely eyes. The young gentleman had a droopy mustache and unexpressive eyes. The girl smiled at the man, and he was spellbound. He came and sat beside her and struck up a conversation. Almost immediately, another man nearby exclaimed, "Wonderful! Wonderful! Eureka!" The second man claimed to be "Bob Miles" of Cincinnati and the girl was his "magnetic girl from Georgia." Her magnetic power had clearly affected the young man. "Millions in it," said the "gray, but large and fine-looking gentleman who had been watching." The designation of "drummer" simply meant that the man was a traveling salesman. Miles was, of course, Mattie's new manager, R.E.J. Miles.

While Mr. Miles was getting the show schedule and advertising lined up for Mattie, Lula Hurst was spending her days performing for senators in Washington D.C., and nearby Baltimore, Maryland. The next stop for both Georgia Wonders was New York City.

Mattie arrived in New York City with her father and Mr. Miles at about the same time that Lula debuted as the star attraction at the reopening of Wallack's Theatre in New York City at 30th Street and Broadway on Monday, 7 July 1884. The unexpectedly large crowd was a happy surprise for the owners, because it was the slow season. The Standing Room Only signs had gone up early on. Mr. R.E.J.

Miles, being a theater man, attended the reopening. He declared to everyone who would listen that he "had a young lady, weighing only ninety pounds, who could do all of Miss Hurst's feats."

Amazingly, just as Lula and Mattie hit the New York City entertainment scene, a third "Georgia Wonder" appeared. Mrs. C. F. Coleman, "the wife of the Superintendent of the Atlanta Cotton Factory," had discovered her own power and, as related by the *Boston Sunday Herald* 29 June 1884, had been showing off her skills at the Young Men's Christian Association. The buzz about the three magnetic girls from Georgia was splashed all over the papers. Reporters wondered if Georgia might have something special in the soil (or water) that grew those wonders in such abundance.

Then as now, the press was not always completely truthful or fair. At times Lula Hurst met with the same negative press that Mattie had endured in Cincinnati. Some called her wonderful and others called her a fraud. But regardless of the opinions, Wallack's was packed every evening to see her perform. Packed houses were all that mattered.

Not only did reporters challenge Lula's abilities, but sometimes people would come right up onto the stage to discredit her. One man, who called himself "Dr. Forrest," was able to do everything that Lulu could do but nobody cared a whit. He was neither fifteen nor a girl!

Lula was described as a "stout, buxom, country girl, with rosy cheeks, small, bright eyes, large white hands, a modest manner, and a low musical laugh." One reporter said she looked like a milkmaid in fine clothing. And fine clothing she could certainly afford. The *New York Times* reported (on July 20) that she had two thousand dollars' worth of dresses specially made for her prior to her Wallack's engagement. She wore a different dress every night during her two-week engagement at Wallack's.

Also that July, the *New York Daily Mirror* reported that R.E.J. Miles had brought a girl of thirteen who had been exhibiting around

Cincinnati. His intention was to exhibit the girl in New York City, but because of his friendship with the Frohmans (who owned a share in Wallack's), he'd decided against it. The latest *New York Daily Mirror* gossip was that Mr. Frohman had bought out Mr. Mile's interest in Miss Price, and she was going to open at the Globe Theatre in Boston. Then "a man named Bullock, who resides at No. 138 West Twenty-ninth Street, in the same house as Miss Price, produced a contract with her parents, and endeavored to obtain a date at the Fifth Avenue Theatre, and also at the Boston Globe. Mr. R.E.J. Miles responded by saying that Mr. Bullock had obtained a contract from Miss Price's father by unfair means." There was no question; Mr. Miles was in charge of Mattie's career.

The *New York Daily Mirror* further reported that Mattie had been seen occupying a box at Wallack's on several occasions when Lula Hurst was performing there. On 12 July 1884, the *New York Tribune*, in an article about Lula's performance at Wallack's, wrote, "An interesting witness of the performance was a young girl of thirteen, who is also a 'Georgia Wonder,' who it is asserted can do much more wondrous things than Miss Hurst." Mattie had turned fifteen, but advertising her as younger, dumber, and smaller made her seem more amazing.

"Georgia Wonder, Jr.," was the article in the *Sun* on 20 July 1884. Mattie had given a demonstration at the Bijou Theater at 1239 Broadway the evening before, just across the street from where Lula was giving her final performance at Wallack's. Frank Courier introduced Mattie to the gentlemen in attendance, some of the royalty of New York entertainment management. Included at the private exhibition were Lester Wallack, Charles and Daniel Frohman, Wesley Sisson, J. B. Carter, F. H. Smith, and "several ladies."

Mattie wore a "pink muslin dress that did not quite reach the tops of her shoes. Her long hair hung loosely down her back. Her cheeks were red as roses." The *Sun* reported that she was not able to read or write. Her father was quoted as saying she had never ridden on a train before her Christmas debut and that she was shy and could not perform when too embarrassed. The *Sun* also reported that Mattie would be at Wallack's on the twentieth. However, that was not the decision made that evening. The *New York Times* reported that Mattie was given another "hearing" on the twenty-fourth to see if she was clever enough to be shown at Wallack's. This too, was a failure. Mrs. Coleman, that interloping third Georgia Wonder, was scheduled instead.

Lula left Wallack's and went on to Boston and Buffalo with her parents and Paul Atkinson while Mattie traveled out west with her manager and father. At that time, there were three other "electric" girls playing at Coney Island and "all museums in town expect to have one apiece," predicted the *Philadelphia Inquirer* (23 July 1884; p. 8, col. 1). The *New York Mirror* reported that R.E.J Miles was exhibiting Mattie out west in early August. The *Kansas City Times* advertised her as "Georgia Electric Girl" at the Gillis Opera House in Kansas City, Missouri. ("Amusements," 22 Aug 1884, p. 2, col. 7). She was booked for "the 25th through the 27th, plus a matinee. Admission was "35c, 75c, and $1."

They loved Mattie in Topeka, Kansas, as reported by the *New York Mirror*. She had shown at the Grand Opera House, "Wood and Updegraff, managers," sometime in August. They described her as having "a very modest demeanor and rather a pretty face, set off by the brightest and handsomest pair of eyes I ever saw." She had received a wonderful reception there, unlike the "rough" reception she had endured out East. The gentlemen in that "committee" were Dr. Hibben, Dr. Moss, and Colonel Stanton, manager O.P. Updegraff, the reporter, and a few other citizens. The "committee" referred to those who tried to overpower Mattie during her demonstration. The "verdict" was that Mattie was possessed of a wonderful power.

Meanwhile, Lula and her entourage had returned to Georgia and visited Cartersville. Her name was mentioned in the *Cartersville American* on August 26 in reference to her engagement to her manager, Paul Atkinson. Lula had turned sixteen. Mattie was not mentioned.

September 1884 took Mattie and her father to Iowa. She was in Cornell Bluffs on the second and third at Dohaney's Opera House, but audiences were small. She was under the management of B. B. Robertson, likely at the direction of Mr. Miles. Her show in Des Moines, Iowa, at Moore's Opera house on the eighth and ninth was described as "wretched business." She had "fair houses" in Omaha, Nebraska, at Boyd's Opera House.

The *Theosophist*, a journal featuring articles about philosophy, art, literature, and occultism reprinted a Frankfort *Kentucky Courier Journal* article from earlier in the year in their September 1884 supplement. Mattie and her power were reportedly "mysterious." Obviously, they didn't think her abilities were humbug.

The *St. Louis Medical Journal* published an article titled "Invisible, Intangible, Yet Real," in their October 1884 publication. "So also in regard to force, there is probably but one force in the universe of a dual nature, namely attraction and repulsion with a great many gradations of manifestations," began the section in which the mysterious powers of Mattie Lee Price were discussed in a scientific manner. "Giving but a brief outline of this Astounding Phenomenon of 'aural' force, or 'odie' force as manifested through this child, a girl but fourteen years of age would take several hundred pages, suffice it to say here, that as far as her appearance is concerned, she is neither fleshy nor lean, but well proportioned, of a nervo-sanguine or cephalosanguine temperament (happy), and no great difference between her temperature or pulse before or after she exhibited. "The mother, sister, and brother of this girl died several years ago and her father noticed; it seems this extraordinary power only last Christmas." This was the first published reference to Mattie's birth mother and only reference to her siblings.

A reporter for the *Chicago Tribune* witnessed Mattie's exhibition at the Sherman House at the corner of 3rd and Randolph, in Chicago on 3 October. Francis Sherman, the founder of Sherman House, was the son of the famous General Tecumseh Sherman. That general was, of course, the same fellow who had spared the Stilesboro Academy where Mattie first exhibited. ("Sherman House" The Great Chicago Fire & The Web of Memory. Web. 10 May 2015).

The skeptical reporter wrote, "The whole 'electro-magnetic-odie' business is a delusion and depends entirely on mechanical trickery." A *Chicago Inter Ocean* reporter was much kinder. He described her as being only fourteen, pleasant with a "mobile face," and with gold and brown hair. "She is evidently of a sensitive temperament, and not of any remarkable intelligence; but she converses well and prettily, and seems to ascribe the stimulation and control of her fantastic force to her mind." He quoted Mattie, "No, sir, I can't do it unless I keep my mind on the object." The advertisement for the Chicago Museum and Theater in the *Chicago Tribune* on the fifth listed her as the "GEORGIA WONDER." She exhibited there through the twelfth.

In 1884, the United States of America sported an even wider range of lifestyle and cultural differences from one coast to the other than it does today. The *New York Times* ran a front-page piece on how horse thieves were hanged in Cottonwood, Meagher County, Montana, nine days prior. "Seven thieves were found hanging to the trees near the mouth of the Musselshell. Over a hundred head of horses were recovered from the Musselshell gang. The Musselshell River, the scene of the grand hanging bee, joins the Missouri about half way from Fort Benton to the mouth of the Yellowstone, and is several hundred miles from the railroad or telegraph, which accounts for the long time before the news reached here" ("Seven Horse Thieves

Hanged" The *New York Times* (New York, New York), 30 July 1884, p.1 col 3). In contrast, the same paper reported on how some New York City streets were poised to get electric lighting and that, while it meant an obvious loss for the gas companies, the result would be better lighting, and "every electric light is worth an extra policeman."

There was a serious ongoing cultural conflict at the immigration station of "Castle Garden," the forerunner of Ellis Island. Apparently, the local spinsters in New England didn't like competing with mail-order brides for eligible bachelors and the authorities were sensitive to the domestic dilemma. "Castle Garden authorities have decided to refuse to furnish (immigrant) wives, no matter how many orders they may receive" ("Contract Wives," The *New York Times* (New York, New York), 28 Jul 1884, p.4, col.6). The cornerstone for the Statue of Liberty was placed on Bedloe's Island in New York Harbor that August.

The Sixth Street Museum in Pittsburgh scheduled Mattie to appear on 3 November along with a "negro who is actually turning white," and "the only counterpart of a Chinese Opium Joint." One could see "A genuine Chinaman…illustrate the awful habit." Admission was ten cents. (*Pittsburgh Daily Post*, 3 Nov. 1884, p. 4, col. 6).

On 15 November 1884, Hagar, Campbell & Co's Dime Museum in Philadelphia advertised that Mattie Lee Price was coming "next week." (The *Philadelphia Times*, 15 Nov 1884, p. 5, col. 3). Also showing at the museum that week were several people from the Barnum Show, the Todas Indians, the Afghan warriors, the Andaman Islanders, and the descendants of the lost Children of Israel. Penrose and Conroy, the boneless athletes would be there, too. *The New York Clipper* listed the acts at Hagar, Campbell & Co's Dime Museum that week as "Mattie

Lee Price" and "a number of freaks and first-class entertainment." Hagar, Campbell & Co's Dime Museum was at the corner of Ninth & Arch Streets in Philadelphia. It boasted three floors, a museum, a theater, and a "gentlemen only" area (Finkel, Ken. "The Skeleton Man, the Jersey Devil and a Multitude of Other Attractions." The Philly History Blog. 12 Dec 2012. 10 April 2015).

A "dime museum," was a popular place to go for cheap entertainment at that time. Initially, the museums simply showcased a collection of artifacts, real and fake, to attract curious customers. However, once that exhibit had been seen and curiosity satisfied, there was little reason for a person to revisit.

The dilemma of how to get paying customers to visit a museum over and over again was happily resolved with the addition of all-day entertainment. The marketing strategy was to charge a very small entry fee, and for just ten cents, one could stay all day and not only revisit those dusty old artifacts but also see new variety acts.

The goal was to increase both crowd volume and frequency. To accomplish this, the stage acts were tame enough to induce whole families to visit, and entertainment was changed frequently so that families would return every week. Acts included everything from musical shows and magic acts to human deformities and curiosities.

During the 1880s and 1890s, circus performers often entertained at dime museums during the off-season between October and April every year. And, not coincidentally, many dime museums shut down during circus season from April to October.

In November 1884, the *Athens Weekly Banner* in Georgia cheerfully reported that Mattie was "A Young Lady Hercules" and was doing well in Philadelphia at the Hagar, Campbell & Co's Dime Museum. (The *Athens Weekly Banner*, 24 Nov 1884, p. 1, col 7). She, "after every performance willfully and thoroughly explain(s) the mystery, so that it is claimed that anyone possessing the same physical powers will be able to perform the tricks that she shows upon the stage." Mattie, as she was portrayed in newspaper reports, was a simple, straightforward girl. She was uneducated, so her ability to pull off her "feats," was surely an intuitive ability to lift and move objects. Undoubtedly, she thought her ability was curious but easily explained. She simply set her mind to the task and it worked, much as a natural artist sees something and sketches it effortlessly. Her manager undoubtedly moved quickly to halt the end-of-show explanations that vaporized the mystery component of the act.

During 1884, "Lula" was often called "Lulu" by the newspapers. By the end of 1884 "Lulu" is all they called her. Therefore, it was "Lulu Hurst" who was slated to be at the Central Music Hall in Chicago. The *Chicago Inter Ocean* advertised her first Chicago appearance starting December 29 for a period of one week.

Mattie made an appearance at Kelly's Front Street Theatre in Baltimore, Maryland, on Christmas Day. The advertisement for Kelly's was carried in the *Sun* and *Der Deutche Correspondent*, a Baltimore paper published in German.

In addition to Mattie's show, the theater advertised a special matinee, the play, "Sentenced for Life." (The *Baltimore Sun*, 23 Dec 1884, p. 1, col. 1).

And so 1884 came to an end. George Price was no longer just a simple farmer. He, his wife, and their five younger children were presumably living off of the considerable earnings of his daughter. Eight hundred dollars a month was nothing to sneeze at in those days. He probably thought himself quite a businessman. Mattie had been catapulted into the spotlight as an exhibit, an oddity, an anomaly, and an object to be examined. At a time when most women never left the safety of their homes, Mattie worked on distant stages in front of strangers and almost never slept in her own bed.

# — Chapter Five —

"GEORGIA WONDER, MATTIE LEE PRICE, said to be but fourteen years of age, under the management of Geo. W. Pike, the veteran showman, then lifted many hundredweights of humanity on a chair and wrestled with billiard cues held by four strong men." Such was the write-up in the New York Clipper about her show at Harry Miner's Bowery Theater in New York City the week of 17 January 1885.

A Hyde & Bohmen's Theater advertisement, published in the Brooklyn *New York Daily Eagle*, 25 January 1885, promised to introduce new talent to the Brooklyn public. "The Georgia Wonder, Miss Mattie Lee Price, who is named the marvel of science and philosophy" would be there, ("Drama and Musical," *New York Daily Eagle* (Brooklyn, New York), 25 Jan 1885, p. 7, col. 1).

Mattie opened in Washington, DC on the ninth of February at Herzog's Museum where they called her "the Marvelous Wonder," and "Greater than Lulu Hurst." She was later advertised at the Theater Comique, also in Washington, DC, for the tenth through fourteenth of February. The *Evening Star* said she "did some remarkable feats of the Lulu Hurst order."

The contract George Price signed with the stock company in Cartersville, Georgia in February of 1884 had been for one year. Presumably, Mr. R.E.J. Miles bought out the remainder of that contract from those "important Georgia men" after the *Harris v. Cumyns* lawsuit was filed in Cincinnati in June of 1884. Miles had done a superb job keeping Mattie booked, but when her contract year ended, Mattie and her father returned to Georgia.

It is important to note that Mattie's act could have brought in as much as $1000 a week, but her contract limited her to only $200 of that generated income. Her manager pocketed whatever was left after expenses. Lulu had kept all of her receipts in the family, and she was getting rich. Mattie's father was understandably anxious to "manage" his daughter himself and keep all of the proceeds; a sum he certainly hoped would be much more than $200 a week.

Unfortunately, Mattie would find an abundance of magnetic competition in her home state. About a month after she returned, another "Georgia Wonder" was unveiled in Milledgeville, about 150 miles southeast of the Price farm. Mrs. Dixie Haygood (later called Annie Abbott) had seen Lulu Hurst on February 17, 1885, at the opera house in Milledgeville. She, like Mattie, had figured out how to replicate Lulu's act. She claimed that she had been aware of her power for ten years before going public. Mr. F. A. Fink wrote in the *Augusta Evening News* of witnessing Dixie Haygood doing marvelous things. His testimony was reprinted in the *Union Recorder* in Milledgeville on March 3. (The *Union Recorder*, 3 March 1885, p. 3, col. 3). Dixie enjoyed an elevated social status, which boosted her credibility nicely. She was the wife of the deputy marshal of Milledgeville. In column 5 under "Personal Mention," it was reported, "Charlie Haygood is mighty proud of his magnetic little wife."

Yet another "Georgia Wonder" appeared in Atlanta. Mrs. Coleman, the same "wonder" who followed Lulu Hurst's act at Wallack's in New York City in July of 1884, made her Georgia debut at DeGive's Opera House in Atlanta on March 9. And if that wasn't enough competition, Mamie Simpson started impressing Georgians with her electric strength in Marietta, just about twenty miles northwest of Atlanta.

While the newspapers that reported on the emergence of Haygood and Coleman compared them both to Lulu Hurst, Mattie was not mentioned. Lulu was, after all, *the* Georgia Wonder, a respectable maiden, educated, sophisticated, and now, wealthy. Was there a newspaperman's conspiracy to simply keep Mattie's name out of print? Perhaps the goal was not meant to be against Mattie, but rather to protect the dignity of the three wealthy investors who had backed out of her contract in Cartersville. If there was such a conspiracy, the boycott did not hold up in all of Georgia, for eventually news of Mattie Lee Price trickled out.

April came and Mattie started appearing in several small Georgia towns, including Calhoun on the first and Rome on the fourteenth. In May she was back up in the northeast, and she was booked at Campbell's World's Sensational Wonders located at West Hanover Street and Willow in Trenton, New Jersey. This trip, an anomaly for 1885, was her only known trip up north. Perhaps it had been booked while Mattie was still under contract with R.E.J. Miles. In any case, by mid-June she was back in Georgia performing at College Hall and Shelnutt House in Bowden and at the Masonic Institute in Carrollton.

Of course magnetic girls were not the only news in Georgia papers at the time. On June 24, the front page of the *Atlanta Constitution* reported a smallpox outbreak at Fort Davis in Texas. A Saratoga, New York gentleman managed to shoot himself when he drew his gun to shoot another man. Of course it was a love triangle. The pope in Rome was to create six new cardinals, and "A Georgia Darky's Arrest" was announced. Singleton Rice was suspected of murder and was "hauled up in New York…" for examination. "Big Bear Lets the Prisoners depart for Home," led a piece about Fort Pitt, N.W.T (Northwest Territory, Canada). "The Crees split off from Big Bear and forced him to give up the prisoners, who were allowed to start for Fort Pitt three days ago alone." The government of Holland had forbidden the importation of rags from Spain and hog cholera was spreading in Illinois. Also, on 24 June, a young Woodrow Wilson married Ellen Louise Axson, "daughter of the late Rev/Dr. Axson." The marriage took place in Savannah, Georgia, and the "ceremony was performed by the groom's father and the bride's grandfather." (The *Atlanta Constitution*, 26 June 1885, p. 2, col. 3).

July through September, Mattie circulated through large and small towns in Georgia working in Jasper, Macon, Watkinsville, Jackson, and Athens. ("The Second Wonder," The *Athens Weekly Banner-Watchman*, 8 Sept 1885, p. 3, col. 2). Not surprisingly, she was still labeled "The Second Wonder," after Lulu Hurst. On the same page is a report of a 120-year-old colored man who lived near Dalton. He called himself Martin Ewing since his first "owner" had been James Ewing. The man claimed to have been born in 1765 in Prince Edward County, Virginia. The man's story was corroborated by the memoirs of his first "master." The old fellow stated his appetite and digestion were good, although he was missing a few teeth. He always drank dark whiskey." Although he had smoked for about 110 years, he had not been drunk for over 35. ("Aged 120 Years," The *Athens Weekly Banner-Watchman*, 8 Sept 1885, p. 3, col. 4).

In Williamston, South Carolina, in mid-September, Mattie was called a "rival" of Lulu Hurst. They wrote that she "is prepossessing in appearance, is fifteen years of age and weighs 100 pounds." Mattie was already sixteen at the time. "In her exhibition here, she succeeded in overcoming the combined strength of the stoutest men the town could afford." Mattie was victorious in the feats of strength, but failed the test for electricity. "Prof. W. L. Lander made a test with the most delicate instruments known to science, and was unable to detect the least electricity in the manifestation of Miss Price's 'power'" ("Williamston Dots and Dashes," The *Anderson Intelligencer* (South Carolina), 17 Sept 1885, p./col. unknown). Mattie spent "some time" in Tallulah, Georgia, in late September, where she was proclaimed the "only rival of Lulu Hurst!" She had given a number of exhibitions and, according to the Athens newspaper, planned "an extensive trip through southern and western states." (The *Athens Banner-Watchman*, 27 Sept 1885, Sun, p. 26, col. 3).

In October, the *Athens Banner-Watchman* printed a most informative article titled simply, "MATTIE LEE PRICE," subtitled, "A PERFORMANCE BY THE ELECTRIC MAID OF BARTOW COUNTY, The Equal in Every Respect to the Famous Lulu Hurst— Her Power Clearly Electric—How the Dudes and Others Were Jostled Around the State-History of Miss Price."

Although the article was unsigned, the reporter was most likely T. L. Gantt, the publisher of the paper. He wrote that a certain Mr. Lambert visited him in his "inner sanctum" at the *Athens Banner-Watchman* and had invited him to see Mattie at the Clinard House that evening. (The press was often given a free pass to shows in order to seduce them into writing a nice article about the entertainer the next day). Since Mattie and her father were already present in another room, they were invited in to meet said reporter.

The narrator described Mattie as "well developed for her age and has taken advantage of travel to smooth out all signs of country life. She is very bright and animated, full of life and fun, and readily consented to an interview." He thought her features "regular", and her auburn hair was, in the light of the lamp, of three distinct colors. "The glory of a woman is said to be her hair, and Miss Price certainly has the most abundant supply we ever saw."

The article related that Mattie had been born "May 19, 1870" in Chattooga, about twenty-seven miles northwest of Rome, Georgia. Mr. Price said he and his wife had moved to Arkansas in 1872, but Mattie's mother had died. "Mattie Lee was always a child of peculiar temperament, being of a nervous nature," he said. (Mattie was actually born in 1869).

The report perpetuated Mr. Price's yarn about how Mattie's mysterious power manifested itself on the farm well before Lulu Hurst had become famous. (Price's description of events echoed Lulu Hurst's father's description of Lulu's "power" manifestation almost word for word). All of George Price's neighbors had heard of her and "crowds came to witness her performances." He further stated that Charley Willingham of the *Cartersville Free Press* had come out to the farm and beseeched him to exhibit Mattie in town. Price made it crystal clear that exhibiting Mattie for money was not his idea, again echoing Lulu's father. However, he said he had been so surprised by Mattie's success that he immediately began "taking in all the towns and larger cities in the North and West." He admitted that he had been "connected with a museum and then a variety show, receiving $200 a week for his daughter's performance."

Mattie treated the gentlemanly *Athens Banner* reporter to a private exhibition in his parlor. Afterward he mused that it "seemed incredible that a young girl, weighing only 110 pounds, could have so easily handled a man." When he took her hands in his, "we… felt a perceptible current of electricity shooting through our palms, and braced ourself to resist the force, but it was needless, for we were thrown around the room as if a feather." He afforded himself of the free theater admission and went to see Mattie again that evening at the Clinard House. He was impressed a second time. Mattie would appear in Athens the following Friday, the fifteenth, and the reporter predicted she would be greeted by a packed house (The *Athens Banner-Watchman*, 13 Oct 1885, p. 3, col. 4).

November 15, the *Americus Daily Recorder* reported that Mattie would be at the opera house in Americus, Georgia, the following Tuesday. Mattie had been at James Hall in Chattanooga earlier that week. The *Americus* quoted the *Chattanooga Times's* printing that Mattie was built like a small giant, only half the size of Lulu Hurst, and she did the tests better. The *Atlanta Constitution* reported Mattie was in Cuthbert on 19 November. She had been to both Thomasville and Valdosta sometime in between. Daddy kept her busy.

"Lulu Hurst's Only Successful Rival Quietly Marries a Drummer," announced the front page of the *Madison Florida Herald* on 7 December 1885. (The *Macon Weekly Telegraph*, p. 1, col. 6).

Mattie and her father had arrived in Madison, Florida, on a westbound train about noon on November 28, 1885. That evening she performed at Madison City Hall. Her appearance was successful and everyone was pleased. There was nothing extraordinary about the Madison visit until the following morning.

George had previously arranged to meet his daughter that Sunday at the "lower Fraleigh House" so they could continue their tour by train. When Mattie did not show up, he went looking for her. When he noticed a crowd in front of the "upper Fraleigh House," he walked over and, "thinking she might be in there, went in." Mattie was indeed inside, waiting to talk with her father. She explained she wanted to get married. Meanwhile, Mr. Samuel Wise, the prospective groom, was locked in the pantry awaiting the outcome of the father-daughter discussion. He was a drummer, a traveling salesman, who worked for a Savannah house. He had also arrived in Madison on Saturday, in time to procure a marriage license.

Mr. Price tried to talk his daughter out of the marriage, but she said she would not finish the tour nor fulfill her promised engagements if she were not allowed to marry. Because it was a Sunday, George had no legal recourse. Everything was closed. After much pleading, he talked Mattie into waiting until Wednesday to marry.

Mattie did not keep her end of the bargain. That very afternoon the couple went with friends to Lake Rachel, just about a mile west of town, where Justice of the Peace T.T. Ellison performed the marriage ceremony. Their courtship had lasted but a "few blissful days," they said. "Mrs. Wise will continue her engagements as far as Tallahassee, where she will retire. She is a pretty, modest and unassuming young lady and the groom is spoken of as being a gentleman in every way and quite well off." Mr. Wise was described as a Jewish, commercial traveler representing Messrs. M. Barnett & Co. of New York.

Courtesy of the Madison County Florida County Clerk's Office

The *Valdosta Times* (Georgia) backs up the story that the couple had only met a few days before their marriage. Mattie had stopped at Stuart's Hotel in Valdosta the night of Wednesday, 24 November 1885. "Mr. H. Wise," a former Valdosta resident, was visiting in town and happened to be present during the show. While he said he wouldn't waste the fifty cents admission to Mattie's show, "when the bell rang up the curtain Wise took a back seat and watched the performance with evident interest." The reporter wrote that "no one supposed for a moment that the electric current (or what-you-may-call-it) which was playing sad havoc with the legs of the young men on the stage was at the same time penetrating deeply into the heart of a silent Israelite in the rear of the Hall, but such was the case." Mattie had remained in Valdosta until three o'clock the next day, and the reporter believed this created the opportunity for her and Mr. Wise to become acquainted. And thus we can determine that Mattie and Samuel tied the knot less than a week after their first encounter. The *Valdosta Times* named him "Mr. H. Wise," but the Madison County marriage certificate clearly reads, "Samuel Wise." ("Wiregrass Weddings and Births Volume 1" by Wayne and Judy Dasher 2000 from The *Valdosta Times*, 10 Apr 1875–Dec 30 1893, Valdosta, Georgia, Saturday, November 28, 1885).

The *Thomasville Times* (Georgia) reported on the fifth of December that Mr. Price passed through Thomasville on his way home, leaving the newlyweds behind in Florida. Apparently the tour had been canceled immediately.

George Washington Price lost his eldest daughter and his income on the same day. He had a wife and five young children at home. He would have had to find another way to support them. Several newspapers in the south carried the news about Mattie's marriage. The *Cartersville American*, so quick to publish the exciting news that launched Mattie's career in 1884, printed not a single word about the apparent end of it in 1885.

# — Chapter Six —

**M**ATTIE GAVE BIRTH TO JEANETTE "Jenny" Leona Wise on 15 July 1886. At least that is when my grandmother Jenny celebrated her birthday. If the date is correct, Mattie and Samuel would have been married just seven and a half months when baby arrived. And even though Jenny believed she might have been born in Texas, Arkansas, or Indiana, there is also a distinct possibility that she was born in New York.

Although Mattie's name disappeared from the newspapers after her marriage, one particularly interesting article was published in New York City around the time that Jenny was born. Almost certainly, the subject of the interview was Mattie, incognito.

The article, "A Magnetic Girl Talks," was originally published in The *New York World* in 1886 (exact date unknown), reprinted by the

*Kansas City Times* (Missouri) in June and the *Fort Worth Daily Gazette* (Texas) in July. The piece is very long and filled with juicy details that point convincingly to Mattie Lee Price.

The reporter, Arthur Adams, said he happened to see a girl walking down the street that he recognized from the "Georgia Wonder" flurry a few months before. He recalled she was one of those "magnetic girls." He made mention of the fact that the girl was untutored, perfectly guileless, backwoods, and with little education. He also noted that her only gift was her peculiar force. Mattie, who was often described as illiterate, fit that description quite nicely. On the other hand, the reporter described her as "still a large well built specimen of humanity, broad shouldered, and with excellently developed muscles." Lulu Hurst was the only famous "Georgia Wonder" reported to have a large build, so one can conclude that this description was deliberately false. If Mattie was married and pregnant at the time, it's easy to understand why she would want to keep her identity a secret.

Adams asked her how she accomplished her feats of strength, and the girl explained everything in great detail. She even demonstrated how he, the reporter, could accomplish the same things without magnetic abilities. Mattie was well known for explaining everything after her shows in 1884, a habit her handlers could not have appreciated.

The girl said she never claimed magnetic abilities, but she had signed contracts to do a certain number of shows for a certain amount of money and she did that. "In the first place… let me mention an important point which everybody who came to witness my performances totally overlooked. I never professed to be either magnetic or mesmeric. Other people advanced the theory, not I."

When the reporter asked her if she was going to give any more exhibitions, she said no. "Magnetic girls are at a discount. They were valuable though while the furor lasted. You see they were something novel and that is what Americans like. Barnum demonstrated the fact long ago." (Since the Barnum and London United Shows had been in New York in April of 1886, it is conceivable that Mattie attended the circus and had Barnum on her mind).

"What do you think of Lulu Hurst?" asked the reporter.

"Precisely what she thinks of me," replied the girl.

At fourteen, she had begun the journey to the hundreds of towns in her path to perform for a period of nearly two years. And as far as we can ascertain, she traveled solely in the company of men.

Barely seventeen when Jenny was born, Mattie wasn't daddy's little farm girl anymore.

Lulu Hurst, the original Georgia Wonder, married her fiancé, Paul Atkinson, in Polk County, Georgia on 9 February 1887. The young couple had benefited greatly from her three years on stage. *The Arkansas Gazette* (Little Rock) reported that she was worth nearly half a million dollars. Lulu's final shows had not gone well, and skeptical, negative audiences had worn her down. She retired and never went on stage again. (The *Arkansas Gazette*, 11 Feb 1887, p. 1).

In 1887, the first newspaper account of an electric girl we believe was Mattie Lee Price, the Second Georgia Wonder, was in an advertisement for The John Robinson Big Show United. Robinson's had arrived in Fresno, California, and the show was advertised for 29 September. A free parade costing $30,000 was promised, complete with hundreds of ponies and a giant horse, boy, ox, and woman. The freaks were listed as Lulu, Tattooed Lady; Jo-Jo, Dog-Headed Boy; Elastic-Skinned Man; Long-Haired Belmont Family; Alligator Boy; and Electric Girl. Lulu, the Tattooed Lady, had been in Kentucky with Robinson's show in April, but Jo-Jo joined later, after his June appearance at Barrett's in Wichita, Kansas. Newspapers rarely listed the real names of freak show entertainers; in fact, it was rare that even their stage names were printed in advertisements. We believe the "electric girl" was Mattie, but there is no way to prove it. (*The Fresno Republican Weekly*, 23 September 1887, p. 2).

We know that Mattie separated from Samuel Wise a short time after she married him in Florida. Since Jenny was born less than eight months after the marriage, it could have been that Mr. Wise concluded the child was not his and divorced her.

In any case, if Mattie Lee Price found herself alone in New York City and in need of employment, she was in a great place to find help. She had at least one rock-solid connection to fall back on: Mr. R.E.J. Miles, her former manager from Cincinnati. Miles was a very successful entertainment manager in both New York and Ohio. If anyone could have secured a spot for her with the Cincinnati-based John Robinson Show, it would have been the powerful Mr. Miles.

The *National Police Gazette* (New York) listed Mr. R.E.J. Miles as one of the "Astonishingly and exceptionally handsome band of gentlemen with whom rests the theatrical control of the metropolis." The full-page display featured a sketch of the top twenty-one managers, and Mr. Miles was number four in the upper right-hand corner. (9 May 1885, p. 9, col. 4).

Mr. R.E.J. Miles
Courtesy of the Police Gazette, May 9, 1885

The *Riverside Daily Press* (California) reported 27 October 1887 that a sideshow tent had been set up on "the vacant lot near Hamilton's drug store." Featured in the tent were an electric girl, a strong man, and a Punch and Judy puppet show. It was not uncommon for sideshow acts to set up a tent and entertain the public when the circus was not in session. The John Robinson Show was in Riverside at the time. The reporter claimed that the electric girl gave off a shock when touched due to the use of a hidden battery. Everyone had a theory. As always, sensationalism sold newspapers.

The John Robinson Show was a big one and John Robinson was a legend. According to one write-up, he was seventy-seven years old and had been in the business for sixty-two years. John Robinson claimed this particular show was, "the first combined circus and menagerie the world ever heard or knew of." He had purchased several independent shows and combined them for this one big show. (The *Riverside Daily Press*, 1 Oct 1887, p. 2, col. 1).

Unfortunately, John Robinson's circus and menagerie ran into very bad luck in November of 1887. They experienced a deadly train wreck in St. Louis on 4 November and then "its consolidated train of twenty-seven coaches was wrecked" eight miles east of Brazil, Illinois, the next day. In the St. Louis wreck, one man was killed and two severely injured. In the Brazil accident, four cars jumped the tracks and burned, but no one was badly hurt. The "rest of the coaches, including the beasts, were saved." The circus train had been making its way back to winter headquarters in Cincinnati. The capitol loss for the two wrecks in two days was calculated to be $200,000 (The *Daily Inter Ocean* (Chicago, IL), 5 Nov 1887, p. 8, col. 2).

It is unlikely that the Electric Girl was on that circus train. Once the circus season was over, the freaks, acrobats, and other circus performers usually went home to their private residences. And while the circus wagons were repaired and repainted for the next circus season and menageries huddled indoors to escape the winter weather, individual performers found work at dime museums and opera houses. Children who had been farmed out to family and friends while the circus was on the road rejoined their parents during the circus off-season.

By 1887, Mrs. Coleman, the third Georgia Wonder, was nowhere to be seen. She seemed to have faded into the background shortly after her Georgia debut. The other 1885 Georgia Wonder from Marietta, Mamie Simpson, also seemed to have fizzled out.

Dixie Haygood (also known as Annie Abbott) had emerged as the fourth Georgia Wonder in March of 1885 but was inactive in 1887. She had given up the stage after giving birth to her son Charlie in early February of 1886. Her husband, George Haygood, had been her stage manager as well as deputy sheriff in Milledgeville, Georgia. Tragically, he was shot dead late in February of 1886, leaving Dixie a widow with two young children and a three-week-old baby. Although the Royal Arcanum Lodge gave her a life insurance check for $3,000, it was not enough to support her family. (*Annie Abbott "The Little Georgia Magnet" and the True Story of Dixie Haygood*, Susan J. Harrington & Hough T. Harrington, Harrington, 2010 p. 16).

In January of 1888, when her son Charlie was nearly two years old, she returned to the stage. Since Lulu Hurst and Mattie Lee Price were out of the public eye at the time, Dixie had an open field of opportunity. She formed a small company and began touring. Women of the 1800s had few good options to bring in money other than doing laundry, selling eggs, or taking in boarders. Dixie was lucky to have such a marketable skill, and she seized upon that opportunity.

23 March 1888 the name "Mattie Lee Price" once again found its way into newspaper ink. The *New York Clipper*, a widely circulated weekly entertainment and sports newspaper, reported her engagement. "Mattie Lee Price, the Electric Girl" was listed under "Fayetteville." She had been there for four nights the previous week and had drawn "crowded houses." The *New York Clipper* wrote that Mattie had left on a tour of the West with her manager, Frank Smith, "a prominent druggist" of Fayetteville, Arkansas. However, The *New York Dramatic Mirror*, a weekly theatrical newspaper, reported her traveling eastward (not westward) and demonstrating at the Grand Opera House of Helena, Arkansas, that April.

The next Mattie Lee Price sighting was in Missouri. *The Springfield Leader* wrote on 16 May 1888 that she was from "Barton County Georgia" and was known as the "Electric Girl." They said she was "small in stature, but has baffled scientists for four years." There was no mention of Samuel Wise or Jenny, her child. They said she had "registered at the Central accompanied by her father" that morning.

While it is possible that Mattie had reconciled with her father, it is more likely that the man who accompanied Mattie was her uncle Harrison D. McAbee from nearby Arkansas. He was a younger brother of Mattie's long deceased mother, Rhoda McAbee. Harrison and his wife Sally lived on a farm near Ash Flat, Sharp County, Arkansas. Francis Marion (McAbee) Sawyer, Harrison's eldest sibling, also lived in Sharp County with her husband, Albert. Ash Flat lies about 160 miles southeast of Springfield, Missouri, which is not an insurmountable distance to travel by railroad. Because Mattie's name first reappeared in print in Arkansas in March of 1888, one can logically deduce that she stayed with her McAbee relatives in Sharp County at the time. Jenny, nearly two years old, would have needed a place to stay while her mother made a living. If Mattie lived with her aunt or uncle, she could have easily taken the train to nearby towns, performed, and returned quickly with cash to contribute in exchange for room, board, and childcare.

On 17 May 1888, The *Springfield Leader* reported that Mattie would perform at the music hall. The Leader quoted The *Louisville Courier*'s article about Mattie's previous exhibition at the Morris House in Louisville, Kentucky. "That she possesses a mysterious power is certain. She can, without an effort, apparently, raise a chair from the floor with two or three strong men doing all in their power to hold it down."

The crowd was small at the music hall in Springfield. Even so, she was scheduled to show twice more at a matinee and perform an evening show before "catching the Frisco," the train that ran between St. Louis and San Francisco, on 22 May.

The *San Francisco Bulletin* glibly reported, "A New York man married an "electric" girl a while ago, and applied for a divorce within a month." This electric girl was almost certainly Mattie Lee Price. While the press gossip was printed at least two years after Mattie's marriage, the nasty tidbit was likely inspired by her visit in June after leaving Missouri. The gossip could not have been about Lulu or Dixie. Dixie Haygood, although dealing with her own romantic drama at the time, would not file for a divorce from her second husband, Mr. Embry, until September 1888. Lulu Hurst never divorced, so the newspaper was not referring to her. (*San Francisco Bulletin*, 13 June 1888, p. 4).

The *San Francisco Chronicle* also published a lengthy human-interest piece on someone referred to as "Mattie Price." This tale seems to have been written long before it was finally published in April of 1889. The article's origin was probably from around the time that Mattie "caught the Frisco" from Springfield a year earlier. The heroine of the tale, whom we shall dub "Street Mattie," lived on the street and was poor and hungry. She said people often called her "the little wonder." She was small, compact and had blue eyes, and bleached hair. Even though "Street Mattie's" lengthy, concocted story was heavily embellished with dubious details, it doesn't take a savant to reason that it was indeed Mattie Lee Price that the article was referring to.

Street Mattie's story was that her father's rival (a Mr. Judson) murdered Street Mattie's mother. The rival then abducted the infant Street Mattie and left her in the care of a black woman in New Orleans. When Street Mattie was three, her original abductor (Judson) removed her from the black woman's home and deposited her with the Adam Forepaugh Show. It was there in his circus that she learned to ride horses. Apparently she was very good but had been injured and could no longer ride. One day while she was with the Forepaugh Circus, an aunt (from her birth family) named Stinsman, recognized a mark on her neck. She was subsequently reunited with her real father, a wealthy man named Mathew Price of Boston. Street Mattie spent two years with her father and stepmother before she fell in love and married a Kansas man at the age of sixteen against her father's wishes. Street Mattie had become estranged from her father and stepmother, having dishonored them. The young couple had been very happily married for two years when Street Mattie discovered that her husband was already married and had children. When the bigamy was uncovered, the husband went insane. According to the article, Street Mattie was working as a nurse in California at that time. Previously she had traveled the whole country with the circus. Also, she sang opera.

The real Mattie Lee Price lost her mother when she was three or four. She was taken to Georgia, away from her mother's McAbee family in Arkansas. She went on stage at fourteen and married at sixteen. Her father, and presumably her stepmother, had not approved of the marriage, which did not last. Mattie Lee Price's husband had been a traveling salesman. He could have easily kept a second family without anyone ever knowing. (The *San Francisco Chronicle*, 21 April 1889, p. 12, col. 5).

The source where Street Mattie might have found fodder for her fabled tragic marriage to the so-called bigamist husband might be explained by a news story printed about that time. *The Osage County Chronicle* in Burlingame, Kansas, 15 March 1888 told of a spectacular situation in Topeka, Kansas. J. W. Jacoby of Topeka, Kansas, had committed bigamy and then claimed insanity to avoid prosecution. The bigamist was from Kansas like Street Mattie's husband, and the man was Jewish, like Mattie Lee Price's husband, Samuel Wise.

There are too many parallel details in the Street Mattie story for it to be anyone other than Mattie Lee Price. Besides, we know that Mattie liked to tell stories—remember the family legend about her running away from the Indian reservation and riding big white horses?

Uneducated, broke, and alone, Mattie Lee Price was only eighteen when she exhibited with Old John Robinson's Show in California. She was still short of nineteen when she reemerged in the newspapers in Fayetteville, Arkansas, in 1888. Mattie had a daughter, McAbee relatives in Arkansas, and a talent for lifting men in chairs. She also must have had the will to survive.

# — Chapter Seven —

THE *ARKANSAS GAZETTE* REPORTED 8 July 1888 that Mattie was drawing good crowds with her "magnetic or electric power." She was a "second Lulu Hurst" and was from Georgia. If the reporting was accurate in the *New York Clipper* on July 21, she had been at the opera house in Little Rock.

The *San Antonio Daily Light* reported 14 August 1888 that Mattie had married. "Miss Mattie Lee Price, of Georgia, said to be the strongest woman in the world, and who has been giving miraculous exhibitions of her magnetic strength during the last week, married her former manager, W. W. White."

The *Arkansas Gazette* provided additional details about the marriage on the fifteenth. "The Electric Girl Married." It was filed under Texarkana news.

"Married—At the Cosmopolitan Hotel, in Texarkana, Texas, on Monday, at 3 o'clock p.m., August 13th, 1888 by Rev. Chas. E. Lamb, Mr. W. W. White to Miss Mattie Lee Price. The above records the marriage of the "Magnetic Girl" to her manager. Mr. Clifford, who has been her manager and who accompanied her to our city will leave for Colorado. Mr. and Mrs. White left yesterday on a bridal tour. The bride is the divorced wife of a Mr. Wise."

(It wasn't easy to get a divorce back then. Even if a woman's husband deserted her, it could take up to three years to untie the knot. No divorce record has been unearthed. The courthouse in Texarkana burned down in January of 1889 and all records, including Mattie's marriage license, were destroyed).

Another, very young, electric girl sprouted up about the same time as Mattie's second marriage. The new girl was from the Denver, Colorado, area. The *Maysville Kentucky Evening Bulletin* reported that sixteen-year-old Lena Loeb had "held a man weighing 300 pounds suspended from the floor in a chair." Stories about Lena Loeb read pretty much the same as those of Lulu Hurst, Dixie Haygood (Annie Abbott), and Mattie Lee Price. Lena had attended the "Spiritualist's camp-meeting" in Clinton, Iowa, mid-August. (The *Maysville Kentucky Evening Bulletin*, 18 Aug 1888, p. 4, col. 3). Had Mr. Clifford, Mattie's former manager who had returned to Denver jobless after her marriage to White, sought out and trained Miss Loeb?

An abstract from The *Sharp County Recorder* newspaper printed on October 11, 1888 places Mattie in the rural neighborhood of her McAbee kin who lived in the Ash Flat area of Sharp County, Arkansas, at the time. "The Mattie Lee Price show was here on Wednesday of last week. The exhibitions of power made by this woman are wonderful indeed and is yet unexplained by our leading scientists. Johnny Bryant, an old Batesville boy, the best banjoist in the south… is with the company." Batesville is about forty miles south of Ash Flat. White and Mattie must have spent enough time in the area to discover the banjoist and make him part of the "company."

As 1888 drew to a close, Mattie had a new husband and she no longer went on stage solo but with a "company." When 1889 broke the horizon, little Jenny was two and a half years old, and her mama was more than seven months pregnant.

Charles Joseph White was born 14 February 1889. A month later, 14 March 1889, The *San Marcos Free Press* in Texas reported that Mattie had given two satisfactory performances at Harper's that week. But not everything had gone well on the tour. The *Austin Weekly Statesman* reported that Mattie and her violinist "came up on the Bastrop train this morning and went south." They added, "She is the Georgia wonder, or electrical girl, who raises 1,000 pounds, but she couldn't raise money and the show is busted." Although she had been billed at Threadgill's Opera House, the show was canceled.

On 2 July of 1889, Mrs. Abbott (aka Dixie Haygood) was advertised in The *Alexandria Gazette* and the *Virginia Advertiser* to perform at the opera house in Washington, DC. Mattie, still out west, would be at the Phoenix Hall in Muskogee, Oklahoma. Lena Loeb, the electric girl from Colorado, had been in Kansas and then went north to Wisconsin, Indiana, Iowa, and Pennsylvania. She was billed as "The Youthful Mind Reader."

Mattie made a positive impression in Iola, Kansas, on 30 August 1889. The *Iola Register* reporter who wrote an article titled, "A Wonderful Gift" waxed philosophically about the inexplicable nature of Mattie's strength. "She talks with perfect frankness and with charming modesty about herself and about her wonderful gift which is as much a mystery to her as it is to every one else." Obviously Mattie's performance strategy had changed and the "mystery" of the force was no longer being explained at the end of the exhibition. The reporter said of her, "Personally Miss Price (Mrs. White her name is now) is a pleasant, well-bred, intelligent little woman." No longer was she described as backward and illiterate. Perhaps Mr. White had helped Mattie learn to read and write.

On 5 October 1889, the *Fort Scott Daily Mirror* (Kansas) wrote about their local fair, "Blind Amos and Mattie Lee Price, the Georgia Wonder, will give their last entertainment here this afternoon and to-night."

On 22 December 1889, Mattie was being advertised falsely in a short article as Lulu Hurst on page two in the *Omaha Daily Bee* in Nebraska. She was slated to show at the Eden Musee that week. On the same day there was an advertisement for the Eden Musee in the *Omaha Daily Bee* on page seven. It included an unflattering drawing of Lulu Hurst, the Electric Girl.

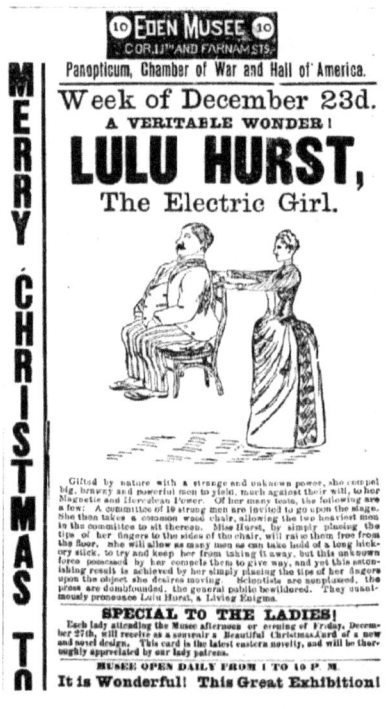

Courtesy of the Library of Congress

A different, but equally ugly, depiction of Lulu Hurst at the Eden Musee was printed in the *World Herald* (Omaha), also on the twenty-second. On the twenty-sixth, the *World Herald* once again advertised Lulu Hurst as being at the Eden Musee. Admission was ten cents. Also on the twenty-sixth, the *Capitol City Courier* in Lincoln, Nebraska, advertised Lulu Hurst as coming the following week.

Courtesy of the Library of Congress

None of these articles or advertisements could have represented Lulu Hurst, because once Lulu retired, she never returned to the stage. At long last, the *Capitol City Courier* in Lincoln, Nebraska identified the real name of the exhibiting Electric Girl. On 4 January 1890, the Eden Musee write-up revealed, "Lulu Hurst or Miss Price, or whatever her name is, gives a mystifying performance." They described her as ordinary looking. ("The Eden Musee," The *Capitol City Courier*, 28 Dec 1889, p. 1, col. 4).

Maybe the owners of the Eden Musee in Omaha deliberately advertised Lulu Hurst even though they knew it was Mattie Lee Price because Lulu was widely famous, while Mattie had yet to achieve that status. (*Omaha Daily Bee*, 22 December 1889, p. 7, col. 6).

On 5 January 1890, the *Daily News* in Denver, Colorado, ran an advertisement for the Wonderland Museum on Curtis Street, near 17th Street. The drawing that depicted Mattie Lee Price was much nicer than the Nebraska ones and even illustrated her winning a tug-of-war with six men. There was a small sketch of the "Magnetic Girl's Home." The home listed for her was "Athens, Georgia," which we know wasn't true. She was booked for an additional week at Wonderland.

In South Carolina, Daisy Robinson, "a little colored girl," had strange things going on in her life. Her "electric" experiences were much as Lulu Hurst's had been described in the beginning, with things flying all over the place whenever the child was in the vicinity.

Meanwhile, on 24 January 1890, Mr. W. W. White (Mattie's husband) was in Indiana. He had stopped by the *Columbus Daily Herald* the previous evening and was "visiting friends in the city." The fact that Mr. White visited the newspaper office and Mattie's name was not mentioned might indicate that he was a newspaperman himself, visiting colleagues. On 30 January 1890, the *Columbus Daily Herald* also wrote that W. W. White was in Cincinnati to secure "other attractions for his show that starts out soon." Again, White was the subject of interest, not Mattie.

On 13 February 1890, the *Brownstone Banner* (Indiana) reported that the Mattie Lee Price Company had shown at Benton's Hall "two nights last week." While they seemed to appreciate her performances, no mention was made of the rest of the company. Mattie's son, Charles Joseph, turned one year old the following day.

On 20 February 1890, the *Salem Democrat* (Indiana) wrote: "Mattie Lee Price, the magnetic girl, supported by a company of refined musical comedy, appeared in the Opera Hall at this place last Thursday night. She is certainly a phenomenon in her wonderful power, which is said, is a gift from the hand of nature, a power she herself cannot explain. Salmon and Whiting, the musical Kings, were exceedingly good."

On 21 February 1890, the *New Albany Evening Tribune* (Indiana) wrote that Mattie and her troupe gave a performance that evening. "No press ticket, no puff," wrote the reporter, indicating that he hadn't gotten a free pass to the show, so he wasn't going to "puff" it.

Lena Loeb entertained the folks in Burlington, Vermont, in late February. The entertainment was partially to benefit the Grand Army post. Lena did her electric girl act and the feats were deemed "verging on the miraculous." Miss Bertha Loeb sang and played piano. "There was a good deal of fun during the evening," and "there was some alleged clog dancing."

The *Columbus Daily Herald* (Indiana) wrote under "Elizabethtown" news, "The Magnetic Girl of Georgia gave two entertainments here March 3rd and 4th. She is a full-sized fraud." That was unkind.

*The North Vernon Plain Dealer* (Indiana) wrote that "W. W. White, with the Mattie Lee Price Troup," would exhibit at Scipio Wednesday night and Queensville on March 5 and 6.

On 13 March 1890, the *Osgood Ripley Journal* (Indiana) called Mattie's performance remarkable. She was going to be at Glasgow & Harding's Hall on Thursday and Friday nights, the thirteenth and fourteenth. The *Seymour Democrat*, also on the thirteenth, wrote, "Miss Price, the Magnetic Girl, does all she advertises and does it well." Here they also mentioned "Salmon and Whiting, the musical artists." The *Democrat* recommended the performance.

A few days later, on 20 March 1890, the *Versailles Republican* (Indiana) reported on Mattie's show at Stockinger's little Opera House. "It was a fifty cent show for fifteen cents, and our people want that girl and those skillful musicians to return next fall, as they promised; and if that spectacled husband of Miss Lee can borrow a better voice, he can come along also."

Mattie Lee Price was advertised in the *Bedford Lawrence Mail* (Indiana) to be at the opera house the ninth and tenth of April. The *Rochester Weekly Republican* (Indiana) called her "simply a spiritualistic medium, and her spirit controls the lifting."

Annie Abbott (Dixie Haygood) was billed as "Strong as Samson" in the *Kalamazoo Michigan Gazette* on 4 June 1890. She gave an exhibition at Ford's Opera House. Somehow she lifted ten men from the stage while they were seated and piled on two chairs.

The magnetic girl (Mattie) was scheduled to perform in Rochester, Indiana, at the Academy of Music the second week of June, according to the *Rochester Weekly Republican* on 5 June.

An act like the Mattie Lee Price troupe really needed to have at least two managers: someone to book and advertise exhibitions and a "lecturer" to introduce the act and sell it to the audience. In October of 1890, Mattie and White put together just such a configuration. Mr. White scheduled the shows and advertised the troupe while another gentleman was brought on as "lecturer," a Mr. Johnson.

3 October 1890, the Bedford Mail (Indiana) reported, "The Magnetic Musical Comedy Co, which F. X. Johnson is organizing here this week and which will appear at the Opera House Friday and Saturday, October 10 and 11, comprises some excellent talent." Mattie had been to Bedford before, but the rest of the troupe had not. In her

company were the Saxon Sisters (juvenile actors) and Howard and Henry Williams, musicians and comedians.

The *Odon Journal* (Indiana) wrote on 11 October that F. X. Johnson had given their newspaper office a pleasant visit and "complimented the Journal force to the show." Translation: the newspaper people got free tickets.

The *Lebanon Patriot* (Indiana) reported 16 October 1890 that Mattie Lee Price would appear at the Grand Opera House with her company on the seventeenth and eighteenth. She would also be giving a demonstration "at the parlors of the Perkins House on the afternoon of the 17th, and cordially invites the scientific men of our town to call."

The *Connersville Daily News* (Indiana) wrote that the company would be at the Andre Theater on 20 October 1890. However, the very next day they reported, "Mattie Lee Price Comedy Company is stranded, and consequently the show will not appear in Andre Theater, to-night." The *Lebanon Pioneer* added on the twenty-third that manager F. X. Johnson had left the company stranded. Without the manager, they did not have money or railway tickets to get to the next show. This marked the end of the "The Musical Comedy Company" experiment and nothing further was written about Mr. F. X. Johnson.

The *Covington Friend* (Indiana) advertised Mattie at the opera house on the seventh and eighth of November sans "company." Mr. White must have scrambled to get her act rescheduled quickly after the disaster in Lebanon.

At long last, Mattie's star began to rise with her show at Geary's World Museum in Fort Wayne, Indiana. The *Fort Wayne Sentinel* mentioned her as a coming attraction at Geary's World Museum on 10 November. On 17 November, the advertisement included a sketch of Mattie's face and a lengthy description of her act.

The Magnetic Girl,

# MATTIE LEE PRICE,

Of Georgia in her wonderful performance of animal magnetism A phenomenon that puz- zles philosophers and baffles the skill of the scientific world. A frail, delicate lady, weigh- ing only 68 pounds, challenges the united strength of six powerful men. She lifts three of the heaviest men in the audience with her open hand; twists a green hickory stick two inches in diameter into splinters with the palm of one hand Stands on one foot and defies any man to push her from her balance Many other mar- velous manifestations of a mysterious power that she cannot herself explain, and the emi- nent scientists of both hemispheres fail to analyze.

Newspapers.Com ~ Fort Wayne Sentinel ~ with permission

For most of 1890, Mattie had shown exclusively in Indiana. Could this mean her husband, Mr. W. W. White was from Indiana? Did he have family there to tend to the children when they traveled? There is a possibility that Mattie's husband was the "pressman" in the Indianapolis directory listed in 1893 as employed by "Wm. B Burford at 174 E. Ohio." This is only a possibility. It does seem plausible that Mattie's manager and husband was a veteran in the field of advertising, because he quickly became very good at promoting the act.

Mattie was twenty-one and her children were roughly three and a half and one and three-quarters by November 1890. Mr. White was just hitting his stride in the game of promoting his talented little wife.

On 30 November 1890, the *Pittsburg Dispatch*, in an article under the heading of "Other Amusements," gave manager Davis of the Harry Davis's Fifth Avenue Museum in Pittsburg, Pennsylvania, plenty of space to sell the upcoming acts at his museum. Mr. Davis has, "no doubt captured a prize in securing the lion slayer for his first appearance in America." Before they could exhibit "Jocko," who ate only meat, they had to build a stronger cage to house him. This wild man was but four-feet high, but he had the "strength of a dozen men." Next, Davis described the other "Curio Hall" attractions. Laselle, the Water Queen, was the only living woman to eat, drink, sew, and talk while under water. "Her only rival, Amphrobroi, the man fish," was to appear with her in a large crystal aquarium. Thirdly, Davis described Mattie. "Mattie Lee Price, who has puzzled the skill of the scientific world for years," was coming. "She is a native of the state of Georgia, is a frail, delicate girl, weighing but 98 pounds, yet she challenges the united strength of six men, and twists a green hickory stick in pieces with one hand." A gorgeous advertisement, complete with the drawing of a beautiful lion, appeared on the same page, which also listed Mattie in third place. Just below Mattie's name was "An Entire Prairie Dog Village" and McDowell & Steevens Comedy Company, the "Two Practical Jokers." They had a lot of interesting things to see at the Davis Museum! Admission was only a dime, and Davis's was open "1 to 5 and 7 to 10 P.M." Mattie's act was listed just below the middle of the advertised acts that day and, thankfully, a notch above the prairie dogs.

The review following Mattie's debut at Davis's was kindly given by the *Pittsburgh Dispatch* on 5 December. "She can sway half a dozen stalwart men by the simple application of a pretty pink palm, and if her power over the hearts of her victims is as well developed as her control over their muscles she is indeed a wonder." The reporter concluded with, "Dr. Flowers, who took a great interest in the tests, declared it as his opinion that the power was the result of an unusual development of animal magnetism." ("A Magnetic Little Lady," The Pittsburgh Dispatch, 5 Dec 1890, p. 2, col. 4). Animal magnetism? Really?

The Harry Davis' Fifth Avenue Museum & Zoological Garden advertisement in the *Pittsburg Dispatch* on 5 December gave Mattie a little better billing. Her name, in all capital letters, was higher on the list of entertainment, coming in at second after the lead act, Excelsior Plantation Singers.

Ever since Annie Abbott, Lena Loeb, and Daisy Robinson started being widely promoted as "electric girls," Mattie's husband stopped advertising her as electric and only called her a "magnetic girl." Several contemporary articles about Lulu Hurst referred to her as "magnetic," and it was better to be associated with the famous Lulu Hurst than with the likes of less talented female powerhouses. One example of someone Mattie might have wanted to distance herself from was portrayed in the *Philadelphia Times* advertisement on 7 December 1890. This wonder was called "ZANDORAROBELL" the human battery. She was the "Gypsy Electric Girl" who was exhibiting at the Ninth & Arch Museum in Philadelphia at the time. "She is charged with animal electricity, and the slightest touch of her fingers gives on a thrilling shock." Dime museums all over wanted the freakiest freaks possible to draw in crowds to their establishments. While Mattie was advertised as remarkable, she herself never claimed to actually be electric, magnetic, or magic. (The *Philadelphia Times*, 7 Dec 1890, p. 11, col. 5).

The *Reading Times* (Pennsylvania) told about a private "test" that Mattie had given the previous day on 7 December 1890. This example shows, in part, the nature of her act and the momentum she was gaining in the dime museum world.

### She is a Marvel.

A private Exhibition of the Wonderful Powers of a Genuine Magnetic Girl.

Pittsburg, Dec 6—A private test of the wonderful powers of Miss Mattie Lee Price, the magnetic girl, was given in the presence of a number of physicians and newspaper men and others at Harry Davis' Fifth Avenue Museum yesterday afternoon. The first was the lifting of three men seated in a chair without any apparent effort. This in itself was marvelous, but not so much so as the other tests which followed proved. A straight stick of young hickory about an inch in diameter was next produced. Three of the most robust men in the party were told to hold it firmly and try to prevent the lady from twisting it into splinters. They made the effort, but failed. She then lifted a chair on which was seated the fat man now on exhibition at this show. This seemed marvelous for one so young and slightly built. The last, but by all means the most wonderful, exhibition was then given. Six men, three on each side, held a hoe-handle parallel with the floor. Miss Price then touched one end of the stick with her palms, and in a moment afterwards the men were surprised to see the handle move about from right to left, up and down, and all in spite of their united efforts to prevent it. Miss Price was born near Atlanta, GA, and has possessed this peculiar power since childhood. ("She is a Marvel," The *Reading Times*, 8 Dec 1890, p. 4, col. 2).

By 9 December 1890, Mattie Lee Price was the headline name, in all capital letters, in the advertisement for the Harry Davis' Fifth Avenue Museum. Admission was still one dime, but now Mattie was the star! Cabinet photos were offered for $1 a dozen. "A life size crayon portrait" with a frame at Lies' Popular Gallery on 6th was just $7. Many performers sold these photos to the audience for a little extra income. (*Pittsburg Dispatch*, 9 Dec 1890, p. 8, col. 2).

Bringing 1890 to a close was an engagement at the Robinson's Musee Theatre in Toronto, Canada. It was a brand new theater located on Yonge Street. *Toronto World* reported on 27 December that more than thirty thousand people had visited the theater during the Christmas week. "First on the list is Mattie Lee Price of Georgia, 'the human magnet,' who is described as the wonder of the world and the puzzle of the physiologists and the scientific world, who, by the exercise of some hidden and unknown power attributed to animal magnetism, and hence her designation as the Human Magnet, is able to resist with ease great physical forces and to move bodies of immense weight." The Prince Yoneda's Imperial Japanese troupe was there as well as T. J. Hetran, a one-legged song and dance man and other attractions. The theater was open from "1 to 10 p.m. each day." On 30 December 1890, the *Toronto World*, under "Music and Drama at the Musee" advertised the same "good list of attractions" for the coming week. (*Toronto World*, 27 Dec 1890, p. 4, col. 3).

Richard (Fiennes-Clinton) ~ Muddy York Walking Tours

The Toronto History website, www.torontohistory.org boasts that Thomas Edison invented the first moving picture show at the Robinson's Musee Theatre. Unfortunately, the building is gone, but a historical plaque was placed on the Yonge Street side of the 1 Adelaide Street East Building. Text from this historical plaque reads:

On August 31, 1896, a series of films running less than a minute each was projected from a "Vitascope" invented by Thomas Edison at Robinson's Musee Theatre on this site. On the next day, *The Toronto World* reported that the "...machine projects apparently living figures and scenes on a canvas screen...it baffles analysis and delights immense audiences." Known as a "dime museum" (admission was ten cents), Robinson's Musee had opened in December 1890 and featured jugglers, magicians, and aerialists, a curio shop and waxworks on the second floor and an animal menagerie on the roof. The building changed hands several times, eventually becoming, in 1899, the first location of Shea's Theatre (later situated on Bay Street). It was destroyed by fire in 1905.

Mattie's name was not mentioned on the historical plaque, but she was a part of the historical opening of Robinson's Musee Theatre in 1890.

# — Chapter Eight —

MR. W. W. WHITE HAD made a superstar of Mattie Lee Price by early 1891. The positive turnabout in the promotion of his petite wife after the fiasco with the Magnetic Musical Comedy Company in October of 1890 was nothing short of amazing.

After the successful grand opening of Robinson's in Toronto, Mattie returned to Philadelphia and the Ninth and Arch Museum. This time the headlines read; "The Season's Most Striking Sensation! MATTIE LEE PRICE The Famous Magnetic Girl of Georgia." (The *Philadelphia Inquirer*, 4 Jan 1891, p. 6, col. 2). Titillating details were described under "The Museum's Big Attractions." She "was only recently back from Europe, where she was a reigning sensation in the principal cities, and was the object of the closest study among the finest medical and scientific men on the continent." Well, Toronto,

Canada, wasn't exactly Europe, but it was outside of the United States and this European implication was good advertisement, even if it was not true. They said, "Although a dainty miss of sweet sixteen, she has herculean strength." Mattie was, of course, twenty-one, but still skinny. Management always wanted the youngest and smallest for their "wonder," and this was no exception. Thankfully, Mattie's husband never referred to her illiteracy as a selling point.

Interestingly, Mattie was in the company of some very well-known attractions in the curio hall that week. The "congress of living curiosities" included, the Madagascar Children, Turtle Boy, Tripp (the Armless Wonder), Fat Nightingale, and the Fiji Island Cannibals. Not to be forgotten was Logrenia, the London conjuror and Mlle Loretta, a beautiful woman with a trained flock of feathered pets. You could see them all for one dime.

Quite out of the blue, the *Philadelphia Enquirer* reported on 11 January that Mattie was retiring from public view once her dime museum engagement was over. This retirement never materialized. One has to wonder if she could possibly have been pregnant but lost the child. It would explain the strange press release. ("Gossip," The *Philadelphia Enquirer*, 11 Jan 1891, p. 12, col. 6).

On the thirteenth of January, Mattie was still the main attraction at Brandenburgh's Ninth and Arch Museum. "Miss Price…weighs but 115 pounds; nevertheless she will select three or four of the heaviest men from the audience, seat them on a large chair and by simply placing the palms of her hands against the back or sides of the chair will lift them six feet in the air. Miss Price accomplished many other seemingly impossible feats and will change her performance every day." Annie Leake Thompson, the armless wonder; Kimball, the Yankee whittler; and Nemo, the Indian dwarf were "among the numerous curiosities and attractions of the grand hall on the third floor." (The *Philadelphia Enquirer*, 13 Jan 1891, p. 3, col. 4).

Mattie's shining success was picked up in the *Macon Georgia News*. It was rare that her name was printed in Georgia. On the fifteenth they wrote, "Miss Mattie Lee Price of Georgia...who took up the mantle discarded by Lulu Hurst for a bridal veil, is now astonishing the peaceful Philadelphia with her feats." (The *Macon Georgia News*, 15 Jan 1891, p. 4).

Wonderland! Museum and Theatre on Linden Street in Scranton, Pennsylvania, was next to host Mattie. The theater was open from 1:00 p.m. to 10:00 p.m. Slated to be at the museum with Mattie was "BIG ELIZA, a living, breathing, quivering mountain of mastodonic human flesh; weight 700 pounds. Also Fiji Princess and family and Azmora, the triple-jointed wonder, the oddest human being born to live." Foster & Rosseau's Musical Farce Comedy Company would be there, too. (The *Scranton Republican*, 15 Jan 1891, p. 2, col. 6). The museum advertised "clean amusement and wholesome instruction" as their motto and the "greatest wonder Wonderland has yet presented, Mattie Lee Price." (The *Scranton Republican*, 19 Jan 1891, p. 2, col. 6).

# WONDERLAND! MUSEUM AND THEATRE :-:

## LINDEN-STREET, SCRANTON.

# STILL THEY COME.

Clean amusement and wholesome instruction
our motto. Week commencing January 19,
1891. The greatest wonder Wonderland
has yet presented, Mattie Lee Price,

# The Human Magnet

A young girl who has an unaccountable power
which cannot be overcome by the strength of
several men combined. She shivers a hickory
stick into slivers by the mere exercise of this
superhuman force, and lifts immense weights
by the same means. Also Sig. Doddretti in feats
of strength; Lenora Doddretti and her educated
dog Lillie; Prof. La Verne in new feats of black
art. In the Theatre — The Fowler's Mammoth
Novelty Co. in a whirlwind of astonishing acts,
vocal selections and button-bursting fun.

ADMISSION....................TEN CENTS

Performances and curiosities changed weekly.
Frequent lectures and performances afternoons
and evenings. Open from 1 to 10 p. m.

Next week—Beach and LaSalle, Man Fish and
Water Queen.

Scranton Republican. Newspapers.Com ~ with permission

The *New York Herald* advertised that Mattie would be at Worth's
Family Theatre and Museum in New York on the nineteenth of January, exactly the same date that she was advertised to be in Scranton,
Pennsylvania. It is hard to tell how she worked that one out, but by
the twenty-first, she was booked at the Doris' Musee on 8th Avenue
between 27th and 28th streets for the entire week "commencing the

26th." She received top billing and roughly 75 percent of the advertisement ink. The Giant Fat Boy and Skeleton Dude would be on stage as well as Rockwood's English Novelty Company. Performances were hourly, and the museum was open 10:00 a.m. until 10 p.m.

New York was an exciting place to be a performer. It was a theater town. There were lots of venues to perform in and therefore there were also many performers living in close proximity in a city that never slept. A most extraordinary event took place in late January of 1891. There was a social gathering of "freaks," and Mattie was invited.

The *New York Herald* wrote a tongue-in-cheek article describing the evening's gaiety. The headline read: "Professional Freaks Have a Reception. Turtle Boys, Fat Ladies and Living Skeletons Entertained by the Tenderloin Club. Even the Cannibals were there. The Leopard Boy changed his spots just to show the absence of ill feeling and the witch of Wall Street was bewitching." "All the freaks invited," led the subtitle. "Perhaps you don't know how it all came about. 'Twas thus: Every "freak" in every dime museum in this city got a card like this a week ago:

TENDERLOIN CLUB, 114 WEST 32D street. January, 1891. The club will hold a "Freak" reception on Wednesday, 28th, at eleven fifty-nine P.M. You are invited."

Some of those who showed up to the party were two fat ladies (aggregate weight 2,193 pounds), the twin albinos from Missouri, Richard Edwards, the Wonderful Lobster Boy, and Little Red Riding Hood, the wolf tamer. Turtle Boy came from Huber's and from Worth's came Mlle Charcot, the hypnotist, and Grace Courtlandt, the Witch of Wall Street. From Bernstein's came the six Morean cannibals with six human skulls; Giovanni, the birdman; and Hickey, the human brass band. From Worth's came "five Samoan warriors in breach clouts; Jerome, the contortionist, and from Doris' came Mattie Lee Price, the electric girl who lifts six men simultaneously." There were albinos, skeleton dudes, and tattooed men and women, Zulu chiefs, and leopard boys were "thicker than dollars on election day." Papa John Keller was the one who had invited them, and he made them all welcome. By 2:00 a.m., all of the freaks had "outdone themselves," except for the snake charmer who "hadn't begun yet." (The *New York Herald*, 29 Jan 1891, p. 10, col. 1).

Not only did a newspaper like the *New York Herald* depend upon the basic principle that humans loved to be shocked by the existence of freaky things, but the livelihood of all the freaks depended upon it too! Humans are innately curious creatures, and as intelligent beings, they can immediately spot the difference between "normal" and "freak" things. We are fascinated by oddities, such as a straw being driven through a tree trunk during a tornado, a dog that fosters orphaned ducks, an albino alligator, or a two-headed anything. It is even goose-bump inspiring (although nauseating) to see those pickled frog specimens in science labs in school. Humans, in general, like the rush they get when they gaze upon something weird they do not understand. We giggle and wiggle and hope nobody notices when we stare at the woman with extra-large mammary glands or the guy with the humungous nose. Some of us call our reaction "scientific curiosity" to make us feel better. Children are sternly instructed to ignore the differences between people; however, our deep-seated curiosity overrides all of our moral teachings and… we look.

"Freaks," as unusual people were called in the 1890s, were well known across the show business industry. They were very much sought after. A good freak could get paid $400 a week, but the lower end of the scale was about $25. All the theater managers tried to get the freaks they hoped would best pique the curiosity of the locals and draw in big audiences. Midgets and dwarfs were always a good draw, as well as the extra hairy. Jo-Jo, the dog-faced boy, was actually a normal Russian boy with a serious overgrowth of facial hair due to a condition called congenital hypertrichosis. He had inherited the condition from his father, who also appeared in circuses. Neither Jo-Jo nor his father actually had dogfaces, but they did look very curious. J.W. Coffey was 5'6" tall, but he weighed only 70 pounds. Sometimes he was called the "Iowa Skeleton" or "Skeleton Dude." He liked to dress up in elegant clothing, wore a top hat, and carried a walking stick (Weird and Wonderful: The Dime Museum in America, Andrea Stulman Dennett, p. 80, 1997). Annie Jones, known as "The Esau Lady," was a popular "bearded lady" and sported a full beard and mustache. When Annie was a young, hairy child, her mother signed a contract with Barnum to show Annie (infant Esau) in his new museum for a period of three years at $150 per week. Annie was a very valuable commodity and was even kidnapped once as a child. There was Charles Tripp, the "Armless Wonder." He could use his feet to do almost anything. Then there were the different conjoined twins. Myrtle Corbin "The Four Legged Girl" was one of the most famous and is said to have made as much as $400 a week. (Pednaud, J. Myrtle Corbin-The four-legged woman. The Human Marvels. Com. 4 April 2015).

James Morris had really stretchy skin! He went by "India Rubber Man" and traveled with Barnum and Bailey. He made about $150 a week. Giants, albinos, and fat ladies (and men) were only some of the "special humans" who filled the curiosity halls. We mustn't forget the half-boys and half-girls, moss-haired girls, turtle- or lobster-boys. Take George Williams, the Turtle Boy, for example. He was only 18" tall and had twisted limbs as a result of parastremmatic dysplasia, making it impossible for him to walk at all. He earned about $75 a week at Hueber's 14th Street Museum in New York City just by displaying his deformed body. That was a handsome income in 1891! He was independent, and no one had to take care of him. Besides, he had his friends and the other "freaks" who were in the same situation, so he wasn't isolated. It is inconceivable to think that he could have been happier being put away in a sanitarium!

But not all of the "freaks" were extraordinarily formed humans. Some of them were very ordinary in body but had a special talent. The "human calculator," is a good example. Although he was perfectly formed, he could do almost superhuman (freaky) calculations. Tattooed people were also normal bodied but looked very unusual because of their highly decorated bodies. There were also the dog, pig, and bird trainers who were normal humans providing extraordinary trained animal acts.

Houdini described Mattie as, "barely ninety pounds, and had the sickly look of a 'consumptive.'" He continued with, "Yet this weakling was able to perform feats requiring super human strength and endurance from either good spirits or the devil himself." (*The Secret Life of Houdini*, Kalush and Sloman, pp. 27–28, 2006). Naturally Houdini understood the principles behind Mattie's act, but he still admired her. To be so fragile and yet able to lift men in chairs and twist hickory sticks out of their hands was, well, kind of "freakish." So yes, Mattie was one of the "freaks" in spite of the fact that she had all of her limbs and none extra.

The people who exhibited their malformed bodies or performed their specialty acts in theaters and dime museums had a lot in common. They were always traveling, spent most of their time working, and would generally be unable to blend into normal society. They were always migrating to a new city, a new audience, and a new stage. Often the only familiar face they encountered on the road was another "freak" they had worked beside at a previous show. (Note that many of the "curiosities" listed with Mattie in early January in

Philadelphia moved on to New York City when she did). They faced similar challenges and understood each other's lives. To each other they were not freaks; they were more like family.

Freaks lived in a culture within a culture, a "subculture" of normal society. Most made a decent living, something the majority of them would not have been able to do without their freakish talents. They followed circuits and often traveled in parallel with fellow freaks from one city to the next. It wasn't a perfect life, but it was better than most could have realized had they not gone on stage. They were utterly dependent upon the undeniable reality that human beings are naturally curious and willing to pay good money to gawk.

Therefore, it must have been a wonderful evening and early morning in New York City for the lucky freaks that gathered with President John W. Keller at the Tenderloin Club. Although these entertainers worked long hours in close proximity, it is doubtful they had much, if any, opportunity to socialize. The extraordinary social event had begun just before midnight after the theaters closed, providing an opportunity for all to attend. And, attend they did in great numbers! What a historic and festive occasion for the freaks in New York City that January when the weather was fair and the temperature at midnight, a balmy 44 degrees.

# — Chapter Nine —

M R. WHITE DID SOME PRESELLING of his wife's act to San
Francisco while he and Mattie were in New York City.
A "Special Dispatch to the Chronicle" printed in San
Francisco related Mattie's success in astonishing the audiences of
New York.

"All she has to do to accomplish her feats is to concentrate her
mind on whatever she desires to perform and supplement application
of her hands with a strong determination to succeed."

Many entertainers had cabinet cards which were sold to members
of the audience after shows. One example of these cabinet cards, is
this photo of Mattie that was taken in New York at Eisenmann's
studio sometime between 1891 and 1893.

Courtesy of the Warren A. Raymond Collection

Mattie's act was, at this point, almost exactly the same as in 1888. It consisted of things like lifting several men on chairs and holding up a chair while three men tried to push it to the floor. Twisting a hickory stick to pieces was another standard demonstration. In the following excerpt from an 1891 article, this feat was explained:

> Miss Price has a stick about five feet long which masters six strong men in her peculiar manner. With this stick she does with six men what Lulu Hurst could not always do with one. She places it horizontally, three men on each side grasp it firmly, and they are warned that they will be driven all over the stage. She applies her open hand on one end of the stick and in a few seconds the six men and the stick are jostled about in a lively fashion, and so shaken up that the men are soon glad to desist and retire shaking their heads and smiling blandly. She also handled six men in a similar manner by simply holding their hands. ("A Girl's Power," The *San Francisco Chronicle*, 15 Feb 1891, p. 11, col. 3).

The article "A Girl's Herculean Power" showed up in the *Pittsburgh Daily Post* on 21 February 1891. Although Mattie never performed in the city at the time, the descriptive advertisement filled two full columns on page 12. Mattie's husband embellished on her past even more so than usual: "One-fourth of the blood that courses through her veins is of Indian origin," he pronounced. And, to make her seem even more special, he reported on her frequent "epileptic fits," which no medicine could help. This is the only article after 1885 in which Mattie's father, George W. Price, "a cotton farmer," was named. Was this the origin of the family legend which included American Indian heritage?

Mattie spent the entire month of February in the curio hall at Worth's in New York. Mrs. Lagrenia was also there with her educated birds and Major Littlefinger and his wife and their performing birds. Birds seemed very popular.

A description of Worth's Family Museum from the Sunday morning edition of the *Press* (22 Feb 1891, p. 4, col. 4) read: "the theater has no doubt taken the place that Barnum's Museum once occupied in this city—that is, as a family resort free from vulgarity and everything objectionable. The thousands of delighted people who visit this interesting resort at all hours of the day are proof conclusive of its great popularity. Mothers and children could not spend a more pleasant hour or two than in making Professor Worth a visit." Mattie Lee Price, Georgia's magnetic girl, was the leading feature that week.

Atlantic City, the only "all-the-year" seashore resort, placed a full-page advertisement in the *New York Daily Tribune* mid-February. One could stay at any number of sea side resorts, and many of them sported "Hot and Cold Seat Water Baths in the House." One could easily reach Atlantic City by way of the Pennsylvania Railroad Company. The Hotel Dennis was available for $3 to $4 per day or $18 to $25 a week. It was only a four-hour train ride from New York City (The *New York Daily Tribune*, 15 Feb 1891, p. 5). Perhaps Mattie and William took a day or two off to relax there. Well, probably not. White kept her booked solid. But it's a nice thought.

Meanwhile, back in Philadelphia, another electric girl, Eva Emerson, was wowing them at the 9th and Arch Dime Museum. She shocked people with her electricity. Oh dear! It seems every decent place for entertainment boasted an electric or magnetic girl to bring in curious customers.

March blew in and Mattie was off to "Bean Town." Austin's Nickelodeon in Boston featured the magnetic girl from the first through the tenth. She "easily held the interest in the curio halls above all others," reported the *Boston Herald* (The *Boston Herald*, 3 Mar 1891, p. 3, col. 3).

The "Electro Infatuation" poem by Park Benjamin was published in Boston on the same day that Mattie was advertised. The author wrote, "Oh, mystic fascination, of fate idealized, I'm but a mass of molecules reversely polorized." The final words of the poem are "One circuit never broken while life and love endure, Forever you my magnet, and I your armature." Obviously, the fascination with electricity and science had permeated the literary world of Boston. ("Electro Infatuation," The *Boston Weekly Globe*, 3 Mar 1891, p. 2, col. 7).

In mid-April, Mattie appeared in Wilkes-Barre, Pennsylvania, at the local Wonderland Theater for one week. (The *New York Clipper*, 25 April 1891, p. 113, col. 5).

Apparently Mattie and her husband road the rail out to San Francisco in late April as, "Physical" Force Phenomena" appeared in the San Francisco Chronicle that May. A reporter related the usual fantastic tales of Mattie lifting chairs stacked with men and twisting the hickory stick, but then he described a new element of her act in a bit that was signed, "Dubitans."

> She... placed the stick perpendicularly and let one man grasp the upper end and another take a firm hold of it at a point about level with his breast. She then placed her open hand longitudinally on the lower end of the stick, and told the men to press it to the floor if they could. Although I have seen this attempted three times by different men, I have never seen it accomplished. The stick will be forced down until her hand comes in contact with those of the man next to her, but no farther. I have investigated this feat so minutely that I am absolutely certain it is not accomplished by means of trickery or confederates. (The *San Francisco Chronicle*, 1 May 1891, pp. 205–206).

After California, the couple hightailed it back to Indiana. Again, we ponder: Was Indiana where the children were kept with friends or family while Mattie worked the museums and curio halls?

"Strong as Sampson" was a headline used in an advertisement for Annie Abbott in June the previous year. (The *Kalamazoo Gazette*, 4 June 1890, p. 1). Apparently Mattie's husband really liked the proclamation, because he used it as the headline for a lengthy reproducible article/advertisement for "Miss Mattie Lee Price." Several newspapers in Indiana carried the story. White must have had a plate made up with the leaded linotype words and sketches that could be delivered to a local newspaper for printing. (The *Times*, Philadelphia, 1 Jan 1891, p. 5, col. 4). Was it in Indianapolis that he had access to newspaper linotype casting equipment where he had (possibly) previously worked as a newspaperman?

The earliest models of this reproducible column included a facial sketch of Mattie and a single drawing demonstrating the lifting of three men (sitting in a chair) straight up into the air. Later models excluded the facial sketch but sported two demonstration drawings. One was of the men in the chair being lifted and another was of Mattie holding a chair while two men attempted to push it to the floor without success. The second variation of the serial advertisement contained most of the original language, but it was retitled, "Strong Mattie Price."

In all examples, the writer of the article is an unnamed "witness" who had seen her act. Variations of the 1891 article appeared in the *Brownstown Banner*, the *Logansport Journal*, the *Daily Democrat, the Evansville Courier*, the *Goshen Daily News*, and the *Rochester Weekly Republican* in Indiana. It was also printed in the *Laredo Times* (Texas) and the *Oelwein Register* (Kansas). Yes, Mr. White had learned the value of serial advertising!

The account of Mattie's talents read, in part, "Miss Mattie Lee Price is one of those mysterious phenomena with which nature now and then puzzles the world. That a girl not yet out of her teens, frail and weighing only ninety-six pounds, should unaided accomplish feats that under ordinary circumstances would require the strength of a horse seems incredible, but such convincing demonstrations of the facts I am about to relate were furnished to me as to preclude all possibility of optical illusion." The heavy men from the audience that she lifted in the chair were called the "committee." If one of them was drunk or someone acted in a way that stole her attention, she would fail at lifting the men. "For, if my mind is behind me and my work in front of me I can do nothing."

"Miss Price," continued the witness, "gave me three private séances, one on the parquet floor, another in the basement where the dressing-rooms are located and another at my own residence. Some of the implements I myself supplied and am positive that deception was impossible." (The *Laredo Times*, 13 May 1891, p. 3, col. 1).

Mattie had little or no education and therefore had no formal knowledge of fulcrum and lever science. The stunts that she pulled off were intuitively achieved and thus if she were unable to concentrate on the task at hand, she would be incapable of succeeding. However, even highly educated scientists and researchers seemed unable to explain just how she could lift a chair with nearly 700 pounds sitting in it.

The "Out o' sight" Musee was opening 11 May 1891 in Evansville, Indiana. They had leased a building at 213 Upper Second Street and "turned it into a beautiful and dazzling temple of amusement, where ladies can take their little ones on afternoons and evenings to see all curiosities known to the world." The write-up continued, "The upstairs will contain a score or more of elevated platforms which will be exhibited in rapid succession all the freaks that appear in the museums of the large cities." Opposite the "freak stands" would be "a row of cages which are crowded with all the rare and small animals of the entire world." There would be all sorts of monkeys, beautiful and rare birds, and "the central figure on the upper floor for the opening week will be Miss Mattie Lee Price." If the folks came for nothing else, they would come see her. Again, she was described as "a young girl," but she would turn twenty-two on 19 May. (*Evansville Courier and Press*, Indiana, 5 May 1891, p. 5, col. 3).

On 21 May 1891, the *Omaha World Herald* resurrected the ugly old drawing they had used in the December 1889 *Daily Bee* to illustrate Lulu Hurst lifting a fat man in striped pants sitting in a chair. They had changed out "Lulu" for "Mattie" in the headline. Mattie was the featured entertainment 21 May 1891. They called her "a regular human battery." This time she was both *electric* and *magnetic* and would be at the Eden Musee at the corner of 11th and Farnam Street. Will Lawler was the manager. (The *Omaha World Herald*, 24 May 1891, p. 8, col. 6–7).

Wonderland houses loved Mattie in Denver, Provo, and Salt Lake City through June and July. The advertisement illustration, one that W. W. White used in several subsequent newspapers, showed a pretty delicate girl this time. Was the really ugly Omaha illustration the inspiration for the new plate? The only interesting point in this series of advertisements was that White declared that Mattie could lift "dead weight," something Annie Abbott had professed publicly that she was unable to do.

The Chicago Inter Ocean, Newspapers.Com ~ with permission

If one happened to be at the Wonderland in Salt Lake City on Friday, 24 June 1891, the ladies got a souvenir and every visitor got a "heaping dish of ice cream." They really understood the value of customer service in those days!

Mattie's only serious competition, Annie Abbott, was being called a fraud in Aberdeen, South Dakota. An engineer by the name of Butler explained to the audience how Abbott's tricks could be accomplished by anyone. ("Is She a Fraud?" The *Aberdeen Daily News* (Aberdeen, South Dakota) 10 Aug 1891, p. 4). "The Little Georgia Magnet," had been strongly endorsed by a list of twelve important Aberdeen townspeople, including the local clergy just four days earlier. "We unhesitatingly vouch for her being the most inexplicable and myste-

rious phenomenon we ever saw." The highs and lows of a magnetic/
electric girl's world were dizzying.

September pulled Mattie and White back to New York State. She
was the featured entertainment at a newly opened theater in Rochester,
New York, during its second week of operation. Manager Marion S.
Robinson had leased a four-story building at the corner of Clinton
and Main Streets in Rochester earlier that year and refurbished the
interior. He said he discarded the idea of naming the museum "Wonderland" because "Wonderlands without number and insignificant
in character are springing up all over the country." He instead called
the new enterprise, "Robinson's Musee Theater." This was the same
name as the Toronto Robinson's Museum that he had built in late
1890, where Mattie had performed at the grand opening (The *Buffalo
Courier*, 4 Jan 1891, p. 6, col. 3; Newspaperabstracts.com). The drawing
created for Mattie's show this time was beautiful—and ELECTRIC!

**MATTIE LEE PRICE.**
THE ELECTRIC GIRL.

Rochester Daily Democrat and Chronicle
Courtesy of the Library of Congress

Mr. W. W. White seemed to have been networking with managers of different serial dime museums to book his wife pretty much nonstop. Once the business owners had filled one of their several museums (and pockets) because of her act, they were anxious to have her visit all of them.

Kohl & Middleton's Clark Street Dime Museum in Chicago, Illinois, hosted a "magnetic" Mattie Lee Price in early October 1891 (The *Chicago Daily Tribune*, Sunday, 4 Oct 1891, p. 36, col. 1). She must have impressed them in Chicago, for at the Cincinnati branch of Kohl & Middleton's, they awaited huge crowds for her afternoon performance on October 19. It is curious that Mattie's husband vacillated between calling her "magnetic" and "electric." Also puzzling was that the Kohl & Middleton advertisement read, "Mattie Lee Price, the famous Georgia electric girl, who returned a few days ago from a triumphant tour through Europe will begin an engagement at Kohl and Middleton's Dime Museum to-morrow afternoon." Mattie could not have gone to Europe at that time, because she was too busy working at Wonderland, Robinson's, and other Kohl & Middleton Museums. Abbott, who went by "Little Georgia Magnet" had in fact been in England (August through October) and stirred up quite a lot of interest. By advertising Mattie as "magnetic" as well as "electric" and mentioning Europe, Mr. White could confuse a portion of the public into assuming that Mattie was actually the infamous Abbott. It was genius, of course. (The *Cincinnati Inquirer*, 19 Oct 1891, p. 19, col. 4).

Wonderland in Scranton, Pennsylvania, welcomed Mattie on 2 November. "The Electric Girl Again," was the headline, and it was not very enticing. The uninspired author wrote, "Her performance is not new to the people of this city, as almost everyone has either seen or heard of it." They must have admonished or replaced the reporter, for on the third, the same paper was more enthusiastic. "SHE LIFTS HALF A TON, The Remarkable Performance of Mattie Lee Price,

The Electric Girl." There she was, being *electric* again. There was also a bird show, a conjuror, a male contralto, a grotesque humorist, and a female equilibrist, whatever that was. (The *Scranton Republican*, Pennsylvania, 3 Nov 1891, p. 3, col. 3).

The world of Mattie Lee Price and her magnetic/electric act had gained serious momentum in 1891. Her husband had found his advertising stride, and he wasn't about to stop the gravy train. If Annie Abbott was enchanting Europeans, Mattie Lee Price would do the same. But there seemed no good reason not to hit the stage in New York in December for a little extra pocket money on the way to their cross-Atlantic adventure! "Gaddah, the elephant man, with his four chins, seven tongues, and an ear twenty-one inches long," grabbed the most attention at Worth's in New York City on the first of December, but Mattie was listed second, "In all her magnetic glory!" (The *Evening World*, 1 Dec 1891, p. 5, col. 1).

# — Chapter Ten —

$\mathcal{I}$N ENGLAND, THE *BIRMINGTON DAILY Post* printed a small piece about Abbott and Price under "London Correspondence." It related, "It is not to be supposed that Mrs. Abbott, the Alhambra 'magnetic' marvel, about whose performances everybody here is talking about just now, is the only possessor of this mysterious new and nameless force. She has at least one compeer in the person of Miss Mattie Lee Price, a fellow countrywoman, who may perhaps be seen giving a rival 'show' at another West End music hall very soon. Miss Price is a young lady not yet out of her teens, who weighs less than seven stone." (The *Birmingham Daily Post* (England), 19 Nov 1891, p. 4, col. 5).

Annie Abbott (Dixie Haygood) had been living it up in London, creating quite a stir, meeting royalty, and accepting gifts from the Prince of Wales.

Mattie and her husband, William, traveled "saloon class" (first class) on the ship S. S. Teutonic from New York Harbor to Queenstown, Ireland. The ticket prices were somewhere between $80 and $150 apiece, with the return tickets discounted by 10 percent. The ship was almost new, having made her maiden voyage from Liverpool to New York in August of 1889. Built in England, it was engineered for speed and was one of the first ships to do away with sails. The massive steamship left New York near West 10th Street, traveled to Liverpool and then continued on to Queenstown. The S. S. Teutonic could hold three hundred salon passengers but there were only eleven listed. Mattie and William must have felt quite alone in the dining salon outfitted for three hundred first class diners. Perhaps winter on the Atlantic was not the high season for traveling to England. (Swiggum, S. and Kohli, M., The Ships List, 5 Feb. 2005, 10 May 2014), ("White Star Line Steamship Teutonic-1889-Ship Information and History." Sitewide RSS. Web 10 May 2014).

Although they traveled in the stormy month of December, the nearly two-week crossing provided a little unavoidable downtime for the presumably exhausted pair. Mattie was always on stage, and her husband was always on the hunt to book the next show location for her. And we must not forget that he "lectured" the audience while Mattie performed. White was listed as W. W. White, a twenty-five-year-old single male merchant and Mattie L. Price was listed as a twenty-six-year-old spinster. Was the declaration of being single for the benefit of making Mattie more marketable? One could purchase adjoining cabins in the first class, units complete with comfortable chairs and brass-railed beds to prevent the traveler from landing on the floor during a storm at sea. Had they such accommodations? While there was a promenade deck encircling the ship, it was probably cold and passengers likely spent more time in the library and smoking rooms than strolling in the Atlantic winter air. There were also baths and "well-ventilated" toilet arrangements. This was the same ship that Annie Abbott and her husband, Richard Abbey, had taken that past August, also first class, to kick off Abbott's London gig at the Alhambra. If the newspapers can be counted upon for conveying the truth, Mattie was under contract to "Messrs. Olliver and Holmes of London" for her trans-Atlantic tour. (The *Daily Courier*, San Bernardino, CA, 25 Dec 1891, p. 1 col. 7).

Mattie's voyage on the S. S. Teutonic ended on 22 December when the ship landed in Queenstown, Ireland. She was well received. Dan Lawrey, manager of the Dublin Star Theatre of Varieties, and some of his friends traveled "by steam train" to Queenstown in Cork to meet her. He was undoubtedly anxious to meet the "magnet" who might attract large audiences to his establishment. Annie Abbott was making a killing in London, and her name was all over the news. Mr. Lawrey hoped for the same result with his magnet. Mattie Lee Price was booked for the twenty-eighth in Dublin. In this first advertisement, she wasn't magnetic or electric, but simply "Miss Mattie Lee Price." (The *Era*, Dublin, Ireland, 19 Dec 1891, p. 24, col. 3).

Before stepping off the Teutonic onto solid Irish ground, Mattie gave an interview and a demonstration. "The Georgia Magnet at Queenstown. Special Telegram: Queenstown. Tuesday—Amongst the passengers who disembarked here this afternoon from the White Star liner Teutonic, from New York, was Miss Mattie Lee Price, of Georgia, U.S.A." In reply to her opinion of Annie Abbott, Mattie was quoted as saying, "If Mrs. Abbott has caused a sensation amongst the Londoners I fancy I am all right. To show you what I can do, I will give a couple of exhibitions here on board the tender." Mattie lifted men and twisted sticks in the usual manner. She was described as twenty-five years old, "9 stone 7 ½ pounds." (That converts to about 133 pounds, much too heavy for Mattie. She more likely weighed in at 7.5 stone, or at about 105 pounds, which is more in line with her historical minuteness). Interestingly, Mattie stated that she had toured the USA, Canada, and Mexico. We have discovered no records from Mexico and only one or two from Canada.

To increase the public's interest, Mattie often gave private showings in order to get influential citizens to endorse her as being the real deal. Mr. Lawrey followed this advertising norm when he sent out invitations to the local important men requesting their presence at a private performance to be held at the Antient Concert Rooms on the twenty-third. She was purported to be every bit as good as Annie Abbott, perhaps better.

"Another magnetic lady is on her way to London. She arrived in Queenstown from New York yesterday, and calls herself 'The Magnetic Wonder.'" (The *Echo*, London, Middlesex, 23 Dec 1891, p. 3, col. 5). Magnetic girls seemed to be the fashion all over the British Isles. The *Pall Mall Gazette* (London), also on the twenty-third, advertised, "The Magnetic Lady; or, a Human Magnet, de-Magnetized, by J.N. Maskelyne" at J. W. Arrowsmith's in London. Maskelyne was entertaining audiences by demonstrating how the ladies accomplished their feats of strength.

*Freeman's Journal* (Dublin, Republic of Ireland, 24 Dec. 1891, p. 5, col. 7) covered Mattie's premier appearance in Ireland. "The newspaper controversy which has recently raged in London in reference to the performances of Mrs. Abbott, 'The Magnetic Lady,' has invested with considerable interest the appearance in Dublin of another Magnetic Lady, Miss Mattie Lee Price." Mattie had traveled directly from the ship in Queenstown to Dublin and given her first private show at the Antient Concert room on Wednesday, 23 December. "Miss Price is a delicate, fragile, pleasant looking lady, whose physical appearance is in striking contrast to the great muscular power which she apparently possesses." She was again described as twenty-five and 9 stone 7 ½ pounds. She was actually twenty-two and never weighed

9 stone. "Miss Lee is accompanied by an impresario, who introduces and describers her various feats." The committee of men who tested her strength on stage included "the Right Hon the Lord Mayor, the high Sherriff (Mr. Shauks), the High Sheriff-Elect (Alderman Gill), Alderman Sir Henry Cochraus, Alderman V B Dillen. Mr. Findlater, Dr. Power O'Donoghue, Mr. Joseph Reigh, Sir. Charles Cameron, Surgeon Thomson, Dr. Franks, Surgeon Wheeler, Surgeon M'Ardle, Dr. Cox, & c." She did the same "feats" as she always did and earned the respect of the reporter. "Now, as to how the different interesting feasts were performed, where by magnetism or trickery, or a nice knowledge and utilization of the natural forces it is impossible to speak with any authority." In other words, the reporter did not know how she did it.

The *Era* was a weekly British newspaper that predominately published theatrical news. The day after Christmas, a large advertisement, probably paid for by the same Messrs. Olliver and Holmes of London who originally contracted Mattie, appeared in The *Era*. "MATTIE LEE PRICE, the Magnetic Wonder... D. Lowrey, Esq, wires: Private show, great hit. Opens on Monday LOWREY'S STAR, DUBLIN, at an enormous salary. Proprietors wishing to make money take a journey and judge for yourselves. Tom Holmes has seen all the Magnetic Ladies, and should know Lulu Hurst was the Original. *The New York Herald* says:—MATTIE LEE PRICE does more with Six Men than Lulu Hurst did with One." Her schedule was listed as follows:

> Scotia, Glasgow, January 11 and 18
> Alhambra, Hull, February 1
> January 25 and February 8 were not yet contracted
> Trocadero, February 15
> South London, February 15

"This famous Artist and all the Leading American Novelties have been secured by the Music Hall Spades, Oliver and Holmes, 20, York-road, London, S.E." (The *Era*, 26 Dec 1891, p. 24 col. 2).

The rivalry between the gentlemen promoting Mattie Lee Price and the one's promoting Annie Abbott was heating up. One authority would claim Abbott was first (after Lulu Hurst) and another claimed Price had emerged long before Abbott. We know that Mattie showed in January of 1884 and Abbott not until March 1885, but bragging rights were key; and whoever shouted the loudest would eventually win the publicity battle.

"MISS MATTIE LEE PRICE V. MRS. ABBOTT" Mr. W. W. White, the manager of Miss Price, the lady magnet, at present performing in this city, writes to us a direct denial of the statements of 'L H Oldham, MD,' which appeared in our columns yesterday, maintaining that Miss Price had been only three years before the public and was merely an imitator of Mrs. Abbott. Mr. White writes that he himself has accompanied Miss Price for over five years, and that she has in her possession a silver cup presented to her by Governor of Georgia over ten years ago. 'I am well acquainted with Mrs. Abbott's first manager,' continues Mr. White, 'and know that her first public performances were given less than four years ago.'" (*Freeman's Journal* (Dublin, Ireland), 29 Dec 1891, p. 4, col. 7). To be clear, White had only been with Mattie three years, and Mattie had been on stage roughly seven years. White immediately began promoting Mattie as "The *Original* Lady Magnet."

By the end of December, audiences were sparse at the Star in Dublin. The *Freeman's Journal* reported, "Miss Price went through practically the same programme as on previous occasions, the nature of which we have fully described." She "failed to satisfy the audience as to her ability to do what she claimed." (*Freeman's Journal*, 30 Dec1891, p. 4, col. 8).

Mattie finished her commitment at the Star Theater in Dublin and then continued on to Glasgow (Scotland) to appear at the Scotia Variety Theater, 11 January 1892. There she was billed as "The Original and World Renowned Magnetic Lady," so as to leave no doubt that Mattie Lee Price came first. (The *Hull Daily Mail*, 2 Feb 1891, p. 3, col. 1).

The *Liverpool Mercury*, on 12 January, advertised an anonymous "MAGNETIC LADY" showing at the Grand Theatre of Varieties on Paradise in Liverpool. She, of course, could do everything Mattie Lee Price and Abbott, of the Alhambra, London did, no problem.

The attendance was good at the Scotia in Glasgow and was reported as "overflowing" with most of the audience there to see Mattie. Her "Sole and Only Agents, Oliver and Holmes, 220, York Road, S.E. provided the *Era* advertisement, along with Mattie's schedule, which was expanding rapidly:

> 25 January, Empire, Newcastle
> 1 February, Alhambra, Hull
> 8 February 8th Theatre, Sunderland
> 21 March, Empire, Cardiff
> 28 March, Empire, Newport
> 15 February, Trocadero and South London

Jean de Henri, also known as Mrs. Dr. Walford Bodie presented herself as another magnetic lady in Aberdeenshire, Scotland, at the end of January 1892. Her husband was the presenter, just as W. W. White was for Mattie. This "human dynamo," as she was called, promised to do everything the other magnetic ladies did. (*Aberdeen Evening Express* (Aberdeenshire, Scotland), 26 January 1892).

Annie Abbott was having a tough time of it as she was constantly under verbal assault by doubters and critiques. Magnetic girls had to be a bit leather-skinned and ignore the skeptics or they would have crumpled under the criticism. Not only was Abbott under heavy critique in London, but the newspapers were pulling her apart in Iowa. "Some Tricks Exposed," was the title of an article in the *Davenport Democrat and Leader*. A full two-column exposé with drawings thoroughly explained the beginning of the act with Lulu Hurst in 1883 and remarked that there were many imitators. Although Mattie was not actually named, the newspaper said, "One of the most effective of imitators and who attracted a great deal of attention a few years ago was a girl of 14. She was slightly built yet strong men were as reeds in her hands, and this only deepened the mystery." There is little doubt that they were referring to Mattie Lee Price. And, "although London is very much taken up with the exhibition given by Annie Abbott… the exposé is complete. The wonderful natural power and the mysterious force, the much talked of animal magnetism is only a skillful application of certain laws of physics." (The *Davenport Democrat and Leader*, 1 January 1892, p. 6, col. 1).

In spite of the abundance of the negative press and scientific explanations, "Magnetic ladies, whilst resisting the strength of men, have a remarkable faculty of drawing large audiences." (The *Hull Daily Mail*, East Riding of Yorkshire, 2 Feb 1892, p. 3, col. 1).

So there you have it. Lots of people knew how it was done, yet the women still drew large audiences. Oliver and Holmes reported packed houses wherever Mattie went, and while we might believe their statements were simply made up to get her better bookings, the theatrical success of imitators such as Jean de Henri (Mrs. Bodie) reinforced the idea that people still wanted to pay to see them.

Sunderland, Tyne and Wear, England, hosted Mattie at Thornton's Royal Variety Theatre on 8 September, and the advertisement read,

"The Original MAGNETIC LADY, Miss Mattie Lee Price." (The *Daily Echo*, 8 Feb 1892, p. 1 col. 1). The reviews the following day were good, and she was described as "very-frail looking." Sunderland is about 275 miles northeast of London. On the thirteenth, she was at South Shields, Tyne and Wear roughly ten miles north of Sunderland.

At last, Mattie was advertised to be in London on the fifteenth, a Thursday. The South London Palace promised a "Special Matinee" at 2:30 at the 'usual prices.' Artistes' Cards acknowledged." A handbill for Mattie's appearance is kept at the British Library, 96 Euston Road, London.

Leading the entertainment lineup 17 February 1892 at the Trocadero at Shaftesbury Avenue W. was none other than Mattie Lee Price. There would also be "AAMA, Eve's tallest daughter, over 8 ft. high, and only 15 years of age. The world's phenomenon, C.H. Unthan, the Armless Wonder, in his phenomenal entertainment of Playing the Violin, Playing Cards, Shooting… with his feet." (Carl Herman Unthan was from Prussia. AAMA, advertised as a giant Russian girl would be in Harrisburg, Pennsylvania at the Eden Musee by the end of 1892, billed as French). The theatre was open every evening at 7:30 and matinee every Saturday. "Prices morning and evening, 1s. to £3 3s. Box-office open from 11 a.m. Telephone No. 5,014. Telegraphic address, 'Samolus, London.'" (The *London Man of the World of London* (Middlesex), 17 Feb 1892, p. 6 col. 1).

The write-up following Mattie's opening at the Trocadero was somewhat bland and repetitive with the exception of the description of Mr. White's role in the evening:

> The gentleman who introduced her was, perhaps, a little too full of eloquence, and somewhat taxed the patience of his hearers by his glib verbosity, but we may at least give him credit for refraining from indulging in what are mildly

The British Library, 96 Euston Road, London ~ with permission called taradiddles. He did not tell us when "the marvelous power" was first discovered to exist in Miss Mattie Lee Price, nor did he attempt to humbug his hearers with tales of her marvelous feats of strength at the age of five. He did not even claim that she was filled with magnetic force. "We call it magnetism," he remarked, "for convenience' sake; you can call it what you like." This, at all event, was fair, open, and above board, and should at once have quieted hostility; but there were some present who had come to hiss, and whose hissing was not to be stayed. It counted for little, however, for the majority cordially cheered the young lady for her achievements, and her success was never in doubt. (The *Era*, 20 Feb 1892, p. 16, col. 1).

Meanwhile, Jeannie de Henri and her husband were entertaining in Aberdeen and Iverness Scotland. She was now called, "The queen of might," and "The renowned and only original magnetic lady." (The *Era*, 20 Feb 1892, p. 25, col. 3).

And yet another unnamed woman in England showed up doing everything that Mattie and Annie Abbott had done. Under the "auspices of Mr. Stuart Cumberland," she performed all of the tricks. ("Society Gossip, What the World Says (What Truth Says)," The *Hampshire Advisor* (Hampshire, England), 20 Feb 1892, p. 2, col. 5).

And back in Boston, "Mattie Lee Charles," another imitator, was giving her magnetic girl act at Austin & Stone's. Her name was so similar to Mattie Lee Price's, there can be no doubt that she was imitating her specifically and piggybacking on Mattie's reputation and fame. Mattie Lee Charles was joined at Austin and Stone's by C. A. Bonney, the albino musical wonder. "Fiji Jim and Annie, the South Sea Island cannibals, attracted great attention, and crowds of the curious constantly surrounded the beautiful engine made entirely of marble." (The *Boston Daily Globe*, 1 Mar 1892, p. 5, col. 3).

Mattie and White moved on to the Gaiety Theatre in Chatham in early March. Mr. Stuart Cumberland and his magnetic wonder from Hampshire, Miss Bentley, were gleefully showing everyone how Annie Abbott's magnetic feats were achieved. The pair was advertised in Sheffield on 4 March. (*The Sheffield Daily Telegraph*, 4 March 1892, p. 1, col. 1). Not to be left out was Minnie Saroney, "The Celebrated Magnetic Lady," who opened at the "Cyclists' exhibition, 1892, winter garden" in Birmingham. (The *Birmingham Daily Post*, 9, Mar 1892, p. 1, col. 1). In Sheffield at the Albert Hall, one "Dr. Lynn, the World-renowned Conjuror, will take a Girl from the audience, and with her perform all of the tricks done by the Little Georgia Magnet." Mrs. Bodie apparently dropped the Jeannie de Henri stage name and successfully entertained the masses in Arborath, Scotland. (The *Arborath Herald and Advertiser*, 10 Mar 1892, p. 5, col. 1).

Magnets and nonmagnets cluttered the newspaper advertisement sections. On 12 March 1892, the *Sheffield Independent* advertised both Dr. Lynn's act of making anyone into a magnetic lady just above an advertisement for Stuart Cumberland and his nonmagnetic lady, Miss Bently. (p. 1 col. 2). Meanwhile, Mattie was still at the Gaiety Theatre of Varieties in Chatham on the twelfth and apparently drawing in large audiences and billed simply as "magnetic lady."

Mattie moved on to Tayleure's Circus on Alexandra road in Swansea, a coastal city in Wales. An advertisement for her show appears in Welch in the *Banner ac Anserau* in Clwyd, Wales, on 19 March 1892. (p. 4, col. 4). She was scheduled to be in Cardiff the following week. Interestingly enough, the advertisement reads, "Mattie Lee Price, who gives exactly the same exhibition as that given by Mrs. Annie Abbott. It is extremely interesting, and if accounted for by mechanics, displays a knowledge of mechanical laws which many engineers in a lifetime have not reached." Mattie's manager, Mr. White, appears to have cleverly acknowledged the criticism about magnetic girls not being magical or magnetic and managed to turn this to his advantage. By 2 April, White was advertising her as "giving an exhibition of dynamic force."

In Liverpool, "Mlle Abbotina, the marvelous Magnetic Lady" was advertised to appear. There was also a Punch and Judy show and the "Kentucky Darkies, Mandolin and Guitar Band." Magnets and antimagnets seemed to be everywhere.

From Wales, Mattie continued onward, showing in Gravesend at Palace of Varieties, located east of London on the Themes River. After that it was the Oxford Palace of Varieties in Middlesbrough, located about halfway between London and Edinburgh. The Gaiety Theater in Edinburgh hosted her in late April.

In Hartlepool (Scotland) an accident at the Alhambra during Mattie's performance stole the show. "Adam Hogg, who was an occupant of one of the private boxes, suddenly leaped onto the stage, a depth of eight or nine feet, and in alighting fractured one of his legs." He wanted to be a part of the committee apparently. A Dr. Morgan attended to him, and he said Hogg was going to be just fine. (The *York Herald*, 23 April, 1892, p. 11, col. 2). From the *Era* on the twenty-third (p. 14, col. 4), we get a better description:

> "He was picked up in an unconscious condition, and conveyed to Hartlepool hospital, where it was found that, in addition to the shock, he had sustained a compound fracture of the left leg, the bone of which was protruding through the skin. Miss Mattie Lee Price, with kindly consideration, called on Tuesday at the hospital to make inquiries regarding the unfortunate young man. He had regained consciousness,

and during a short conversation that she had with him he blamed no one but himself for the untoward occurrence."

There was "A Great Triple Bill at the Dime Museum This Week" of 25 April 1892 in Philadelphia at the 9th and Arch Museum where Mattie had previously been well received. The Wonderful Zarros would be there, and they would cut off a man's head in "full view of the audience." Texas Ben, the daring scout, and his wife, Texas Ann, both of whom were in the recent terrible Indian battle at Wounded Knee would have on display a valuable collection of relics and war implements. 9th and Arch Museum also promised, "Something that will delight the thousands of children who flock to the Museum is the miniature skating rink, which occupied the inventor seventeen years in its construction, and cost $10,000. Among a host of other interesting freaks are Zumegas, the Circassian beauty, the only living mermaid, and Eva Emerson, the electric girl." Admission was still a dime.

"There is no business more thoroughly cut and dried than that of the exhibition of freaks." Everyone in every museum across the country knew the real freaks, not the fabricated ones, but the *real* ones. Those honest-to-goodness human oddities had a certain proud standing in the community. The real freaks or classic freaks received a fixed salary for showing their "misshapen selves" and breathing "the foul air of a museum for 12 hours a day." In talking about these freaks, one usually gets "startling facts, such as "Stewart, the truncated fraction of humanity, is playing in Cleveland." And that the "electricity in Mattie Palmer, the magnetic girl, gave out Friday… Millie Christine, the two-headed nightingale, who was a contemporary of Booth and Barrett, and occupied about the same position in the freak business as they did in the theatrical firmament, is said to have received four hundred dollars per week." The humans who have suffered tragedy, such as bad burns or the like, were not considered genuine. (The *Morning Star* (Rockford, IL), 17 Mar 1892, p. 3).

And all the freaks traveled because once an audience got used to seeing their anomalies, they were no longer interesting. Mattie Lee Price was considered one of the freaks, and it was time for her to hit the trail again. She and William left England and traveled home. The arrival papers show the trip was from Liverpool to New York on the Etruria. It docked on 16 May 1892. This time the pair was listed as William and Mattie White, married. They listed their last residence as London and their citizenships as United States. He was recorded as twenty-nine and Mattie twenty-four but she would not even turn twenty-three until three days later. They had five pieces of luggage. (Year: 1892, arrival: New York, New York, microfilm serial: M237, 1820–1897, microfilm roll: roll 588, line: 1, page number: 22).

# — Chapter Eleven —

N O EVIDENCE HAS SURFACED TO indicate where Mattie was between mid-May of 1892 and mid-October when the serial advertisement, "Strong as Samson," once again heralded her performance in the *Morning Star* newspaper in Rockfort, Illinois. (14 Oct 1892, p. 2, col. 2). However, given her history of almost continuous employment, it seems unlikely she took a five-month vacation. Instead, she probably worked the summer months as part of a traveling circus, anonymously left out of circus advertisements.

On 17 October 1892, an advertisement for Cincinnati's "Kohl & Middleton's Mammoth Dime Museum and Family Theater" announced that "Mattie Lee Price, Magnetic Girl" would be coming the following week. Also anticipated was "Count Ivan Dorschky Orloff, the Living Ossified Transparent Man." Poor Ivan had a wasting disease, which caused his bones to be so weak they bent easily (quite the opposite of ossified) and made his skin so thin that the blood could be seen coursing through his veins.

Also in October, Annie Abbott (Mattie's only real competition) suffered a disheartening setback. She was "hissed at" in Berne, Switzerland, and the police had to come to her rescue. She immediately canceled the rest of her Swiss tour. (The *Roanoke Times*, 20 Oct 1892, p. 4, col. 3).

The pretty little drawing of Mattie lifting three men in a chair, the same advertisement that had beckoned customers to the Wonderland Museum in Denver in 1891, was resurrected and reused as a Kohl & Middleton advertisement in Cincinnati on 23 October. (The *Cincinnati Enquirer*, 23 Oct 1892, p. 19, col. 4). On the twenty-fourth, the *Enquirer* described Mattie's act in detail and proclaimed this to be her first appearance since her "triumphant tour of Europe." By 29 October, "Electra, the wonderful new electric girl" graced the Cincinnati stage along with the Ossified Man. Miss Mattie Lee Price had moved on.

Mattie seemingly disappeared after October 1892. A quick search of western newspapers rendered many sightings of various "Georgia Wonders" and "Little Georgia Magnets," but those found thus far have all proved to be someone other than Mattie. Was she in Canada, Mexico, somewhere out west, or in some foreign land where information is less accessible?

When May 1893 rolled around, the national mood of the American people was similar to what Charles Dickens so aptly described it in *The Tale of Two Cities* in 1859: "It was the best of times, it was the worst of times, it was the age of wisdom, it was the age of foolishness, it was the epoch of belief, it was the epoch of incredulity, it was the season of Light, it was the season of Darkness, it was the spring of hope, it was the winter of despair, we had everything before us, we had nothing before us, we were all going direct to Heaven, we were all going direct the other way." (Dickens, C. (1859) *A Tale of Two Cities. London, England: James Nisbet & Co, Limited).*

The worst of 1893 was the American economy, which spiraled down rapidly into deep financial depression. The US gold reserves were at an all-time low, mostly because of some unfortunate legislation that passed in 1890. The law had tied the value of silver to gold in a direct ratio. Silver rapidly became exponentially more abundant as that tempting new valuation spurred more mining. In a free market, the value of silver would have fallen naturally as supply increased, but the legislation that tied the value of silver to gold kept the silver value artificially high. Astute investors traded their abundant fixed-value silver holdings for government held gold. This rush to exchange silver for gold depleted the US gold reserves alarmingly. President Cleveland repealed the "Silver Purchase Act" of 1890 as soon as he took office in 1893, but it was too late. The panic caused by the depleted gold reserves was the beginning of a deep depression resulting in the closure of over five hundred banks and at least fifteen thousand businesses. Prices on Wall Street and Main Street plummeted and labor wages declined. The overall economy shrank. Unemployment soared to 35 percent in New York. Even the hugely popular and exceedingly successful Reading Railroad managed to overextend itself and was forced to file bankruptcy. Investors lost heavily. Theaters and dime museums had to decrease prices to entice customers, no doubt resulting in smaller profits and less pay for entertainers like Mattie.

In the midst of the fear and sorrow caused by the deepening financial crisis, there arose a grand and enormous fair. The World Columbian Exposition opened on 1 May 1893 in Chicago, Illinois. It was a masterpiece built against impossible odds and at great cost.

This, Chicago's pride and triumph, showcased much of what was good in society. Science, architecture, culture, and society were expanding in positive and marvelous directions, and the masses flocked from all over the world to see, learn, and experience all the latest innovations. Without a doubt The World Columbian Exposition epitomized the very best of times for 1893.

Perhaps the extravaganza should have opened in October of 1892 to commemorate exactly four hundred years since Columbus "sailed the ocean blue" and discovered the Americas. However, it could be said that the fair opened just in time, just as the panic of 1893 held the nation firmly in its grip. It acted as a sort of counterbalance to the horrors of financial ruin and feelings of hopelessness. It was an enormously beautiful exposition filled with ideas, hope, and, of course, fun.

More than twenty-seven million visitors paid to visit the World Columbian Exposition. They came from all over the globe to be a part of the six-month-long extravaganza. Gentlemen with walking sticks clad in dark, three-piece suits and crowned in bowler hats escorted ladies turned out in long black dresses with their ever-present parasols. Wheelchairs were offered for invalids. The chair with an attendant was seventy cents per hour, but would cost only forty cents without one. Bordering Lake Michigan and sprawling over six hundred acres, the fair was grand entertainment for the fifty-cent entrance fee.

There were paved streets, landscaped gardens, fountains, and beautiful canals and bridges. The specially designed (temporary) buildings that housed the plentiful exhibits were, in fact, architectural masterpieces covered in elegantly simple white stucco. Electricity pulsed throughout the exposition, showcasing cutting edge technology. Thomas A. Edison's company, General Electric, had proposed DC current usage. However, Edison lost the contract to George Westinghouse, who proposed using, at a significantly lower cost, the AC or alternating current system developed by Nikola Tesla.

The "Women's Building" was designed, built, and run entirely by women to showcase and elevate women in modern society. While some embraced and applauded the concept, many more boycotted it altogether. The majority of men still believed women incapable of accomplishing anything outside of the home in 1893, and they were against anything that would encourage women in that direction. It would be another twenty-three years before women even won the right to vote.

Other buildings housed exhibitions in areas of agriculture, electricity, mining, fisheries, forestry, and liberal arts, just to name a few. Every state was represented and several countries. The expanse of pure white buildings and an abundance of street lighting made this temporary city sparkle. It was quickly dubbed "The White City." (Unfortunately, some believed that "white" referred to race rather than building color and considered the nickname racist).

A few of the inventions sampled at the exposition were Shredded Wheat, Juicy Fruit gum, Cracker Jack, and Pabst (Blue Ribbon) Beer. The first cream of wheat, diet soda, and prepackaged pancake mix by Aunt Jemima also debuted. The first publicly shown zipper zipped and Ferris's first big wheel at 250 feet in diameter, turned around and around. Scott Joplin, an ingenious African American musician and composer, unleashed his joyful ragtime style of piano music, adding an unforgettable upbeat tempo to the festive occasion.

There were special events and parades with lively music that celebrated the diverse cultures taking part in the fair. Even Buffalo Bill (who set up his show just outside of the official grounds) and his Congress of Rough Riders were allowed to lead the parade toward the end of the exposition. The 'pomp and circumstance' was wonderful, colorful, and loud.

The Midway Plaisance, a wide stretch of land about a mile long that connected Washington Park to Jackson Park (where the exposition was situated), was often the most memorable for fair goers. Although the exposition planners had hoped visitors would experience sober, educational insight into the foreign cultures exhibited along the Midway, it turned into something more like a carnival.

Set apart from the sophisticated scientific exhibits of the exposition proper, the Midway evolved into a joyful playground. Rides of two full revolutions on the enormous Ferris wheel were offered for fifty cents. It was new, novel, and worth every penny to be taken high enough to see the whole expositional splendor from above. Besides the wheel, there were over fifty tents and huts planted along the Midway. The variety of things to see was extraordinary and diverse! There were living cultural experiences, such as foreign shows in theaters and exotic places to eat and drink. There were tents lined with photographs of lands far away, places the visitors could never dream of seeing in person. The entertainment was mysterious, exciting, and sometimes even offensive to prudish fair goers. One entertainer given the moniker, "Little Egypt," was a favorite attraction. She is credited with introducing "belly dancing" to the American public in an area of the Midway called The Streets of Cairo. Highly criticized by the religious crowd, it proved to be a most popular attraction for the gentlemen.

All of the things to see, ride, drink, and eat on the Midway Plaisance required their own admission fee, but there were package deals even then. One advertisement read, "The Turkish restaurant, native musical performances, tribe of Bedouins, admission 25 cents." (The *Barton County Democrat* (Great Bend, Kansas), 25 May 1893, p. 3, col. 4).

Entertainers along the Midway were not always from the countries they pretended to hail from. Not all were as authentic as "Little Egypt." One such masquerader was Harry Houdini. He and his brother dressed themselves as "dark-skinned yogis" and performed a magic seed-growing act on the Midway. They "passed the hat" after their show instead of charging an admission. (*The Secret Life of Houdini*, William Kalush and Larry Sloman, ATRIA Books, 2006, p. 25). With all of those curious fairgoers eager to be entertained, there was plenty of incentive for entertainers like Houdini to dress up and play whatever part necessary to make a dollar. Did Mattie Lee Price perform at the 1893 world fair? Probably. We believe so, but who could possibly know all of the names of the hundreds of entertainers who put on a show, incognito, on the Midway Plaisance in Chicago between 1 May and 30 October 1893?

Eleven months after her Cincinnati show at Kohl & Middleton's (October 1892), Mattie's name once again appeared in the newspapers. She was listed as a coming attraction for Kohl & Middleton's Euclid Avenue Dime Museum in Cleveland, Ohio. "Miss Mattie Lee Price, known as 'the Georgia Magnetic Wonder'" was expected on 26 September 1893. She was described as a "slight, girlish prodigy, who weighs less than 120 pounds." (th*e Cleveland Leader*, 26 Sept 1893). An advertisement in the Cleveland Leader on 24 September shows a delicate Mattie lifting three men right up into the air!

Courtesy of the John F. Polacsek Collection

After the Cleveland engagement, Mattie returned to Kohl & Middleton's in Cincinnati, opening on 2 October. (The *Cincinnati Enquirer*, 1 Oct 1893, p. 19, col. 3).

On 22 October 1893, The *Daily Inter Ocean* of Chicago, Illinois, printed an advertisement for Kohl & Middleton's South Clark Street dime museum (sec. 3, p. 25, col. 4). Listed as the week's "principle attractions in the main curio halls" were "Mattie Lee Price, the Georgia magnetic girl; the Houdin brothers; French illusionists: Gilbert and his wife, the Texas giant and giantess, and others." Harry Houdini was, at this time, still listed as "Houdin" and his brother was still his assistant.

The principal attractions in the main curi⟨
halls of Kohl & Middleton's South Clark stree⟨
dime museum during the week will consist o
Mattie Lee Price, the Georgia magnetic girl; th⟨
Houdin brothers; French illusionists: Gilber
and his wife, the Texas giant and giantess, an⟨
others. Sanderlin's living statues will be seer
hourly in theater No. 1, Moor's Irish Senators i⟨
theater No. 2, and Davis and Barrett's Vaudeville⟨
in theater No. 3.

Harry Houdini (born Erik Weisz) wrote in 1920 about being billed with Mattie during this particular time period, i.e., "twenty-six years ago." Of Mattie he wrote, "I was on the bill with Mattie Lee Price, who though less well known, was in many ways superior to either Miss Hurst or Miss Abbott." But while he admired Mattie's expertise, it was her husband's ability to sell the act that got his attention. Of Mr. White, he wrote, "He "sold" the act as no other man has sold an act before or since." Key to the success of any performer was the selling of the performance.

Houdini wrote that he was next billed alongside Mattie in "Burton's Museum, Milwaukee; but when we made the next jump I found that White was not along." Undoubtedly Houdini knew more about the situation but he simply wrote, "They had had a family squabble, the other apex of the triangle being a circus grafter who 'shibbolethed' at some of the 'brace games,' which at that time had police protection, so far as that could be given. He had interfered between the couple, and was, I am sorry to say, quite successful as an interferer." (www. gutenberg.org/files/435/435-h/435-h.htm, links to The Miracle Mongers and Their Methods, An Exposé, Harry Houdini, Google Books [EBook #435], 1920, pp. 27–28).

What really caused the breakup of what seemed to be a successful symbiotic couple? Could the tensions of the economic downturn have fractured the marriage? Did White invest Mattie's considerable earnings from the lucrative years into stock that crashed leaving them broke? Had Mattie simply fallen in love with a man she met at the fair?

The Chicago World Columbian Exposition was scheduled to end on 30 October 1893. An elaborate celebration was planned but all festivities were abruptly canceled. Carter Harrison, the mayor of Chicago, was murdered in his own home on the evening of the twenty-eighth. A memorial ceremony in honor of the mayor took the place of the planned closing celebration. Patrick Prendergast, the man who shot the mayor, was hung in 1894. Buffalo Bill put on one last show there on the thirty-first. The party was over in Chicago (Assassination of Carter Harrison. (n.d.).

Retrieved May 17, 2016, from: www.encyclopedia.chicagohistory. org/pages/2386.html.(The Daily Inter Ocean (Chicago, IL), 22 Oct 1893, sec. 3, p. 25).

# — Chapter Twelve —

O N NEW YEAR'S EVE 1893, Mattie performed at Frank Hall's
Casino in Chicago, Illinois. The advertisement for Hall's that
day was enormous, included a number-puzzle, and was filled
with the promise of wonderful entertainment. "A WONDER: A
MARVELOUS DELIGHT! Crowded at all hours and "the curtain
never drops" for 12 consecutive hours. TODAY, TOMORROW,
EVERY DAY every day from 11 a.m. to 11 p.m." A list of the new
talent was proudly announced which included cloggers, musicians,
comedians, twins, "'Mysterious Gaza," Magnetic Wonder and 50
others.'" (The *Sunday Inter Ocean*, 31 Dec 1893, p. 11, col. 6).

On 2 January 1894, Frank Hall's Casino advertised "Gaza," but
this time the theater manager invited physicians from the city to be
on the committee and test her extraordinary powers.

THE BALANCING TEST.

Chicago Tribune, Newspapers.com ~ with permission

Chicago Tribune, Newspapers.com ~ with permission

Once again Hall's advertisement trumpeted Mattie's recent European tour, but instead of calling her "Mattie Lee Price," they again called her "The Mysterious Gaza!" Since Mattie was well known in dime museum and theater circles, was the name change a simple ploy to make her act seem fresh, new and, of course, mysterious?

Why did she choose Mysterious Gaza as a stage name? While once or twice she had been falsely advertised as Lulu Hurst, otherwise she had always been billed simply as Mattie Lee Price with one or another magnetic or electric pronoun. The word "Gaza" is generally associated with an area in Palestine, a few places in South Africa, and a village in New Hampshire, none of which seem to have any connection to a lightweight twenty-five-year-old woman with enormous stage strength.

Recalling that Harry Houdini professed to cloaking himself (and his brother) in the role of a "dark-skinned yogi" in order to perform his illusions on the Midway Plaisance, it begins to make sense; if Houdini pulled off pretending to be someone else at the tender age of nineteen, couldn't gray-eyed Mattie have done something similar? Had she also occupied a small piece of that lucrative real estate on the Midway Plaisance as the Mysterious Gaza, a Middle Eastern wonder? Probably. Was it there that the tall, dark stranger lured her from her husband of five years? Possibly.

While Mattie was successfully entertaining large audiences in Chicago in January of 1894, a Chicago man by the name of Herman Webster Mudget, aka Dr. Henry Howard Holmes, was on his way to Texas to claim a fortune that wasn't really his. Mr. H. H. Holmes was a Chicago serial killer who had built a block long building people dubbed "the castle" at 601–603 West 63rd Street in the Englewood neighborhood. Located less than four miles (and a straight shot on the railway) from the 1893 World Columbian Exposition in Jackson Park, Holmes had offered rooms in his house of horrors to unsuspecting, mostly female, exposition visitors. It was rumored Holmes killed as many as two hundred people, including women, children, and unborn babies. In the basement of his castle, he cremated some of the bodies in a specially built furnace and others he simply dissolved in a large vat of lye.

He stripped the flesh from several victims and sold their skeletons to medical students and institutions. Remarkably, authorities did not question the dead bodies found in his possession because Holmes had declared himself both a doctor and pharmacist. It was not unusual for deceased patients to be left with a doctor. Holmes was also an exceedingly charming, blue-eyed bigamist. Holmes committed innumerable acts of financial fraud, the latest of which (in early 1894) had drawn him to Fort Worth, Texas. His so-called castle burned down in 1895. He was hung in 1896 in Philadelphia for killing his partner in crime, Benjamin Pitezel.

Mattie could easily have crossed paths with the killer. She had been at Kohl & Middleton's at 263 W 63rd Street in October 1893, just seven miles from Holmes's murder house. When she was at Frank Hill's Casino, she was just one mile further away on Wabash Avenue near Jackson Street. And, of course, Mattie was at the exposition that summer, just four miles from the monster's lair. She was young and pretty and just his type. Holmes's had a pharmacy located on the ground floor of his bizarrely constructed building. The pharmacy was well advertised and very popular. Mattie had left her husband, W.W. White, right in the middle of the murderer's reign in Chicago. This had to be a stressful time for her, changing husbands and all. Might she have dropped by the store for one of Holmes's famous tonics to treat her stress?

Although the psychopath had kidnapped and killed other women (and their children), thankfully Mattie was not caught in his diabolic snare. (*The Devil in the White City: Murder, Magic, and Madness at the Fair That Changed America*, Erick Larson, 2003).

So rather than melting anonymously in a vat of lye in Holmes's basement, Mattie continued to amaze the people of Chicago at Frank Hall's Casino in early 1894. *The Chicago Inter Ocean* ("General Mention," 3 Jan 1894, p. 6, col. 6) described Mattie's act in five parts. She could lift one man in a chair without actually gripping the chair. She could prevent a party of two men from placing a stick on the ground. She was able to lift three men in a chair. She could create enough torque on a hickory stick to twist it out of the hands of the three men holding it. And, finally, she could resist the efforts of six men trying to place one end of the stick on the floor. (There were a couple of other stunts that she could do, but the reporter seemed to like his organized five-point description as it was). Admission was ten, fifteen, twenty-five, or fifty cents.

"FRANK HALL'S CASINO (formerly Haverly's)" was advertised as a resort for men, women, and children. After the establishment changed hands, the new owners made many improvements. There was a new "café and restaurant for ladies… on the main upper floor, and a large orchestra… placed on the lower floor." (The *Sunday Inter Ocean*, 7 Jan 1894, p. 29, col. 4).

"The Mystery of a Woman" was sprawled in large print across a full column and a half of page 26 of the *Chicago Tribune* on 7 January (p. 26, col. 4–5). Described was Mattie as "22 years old" (although she was nearly twenty-five) and only 90 pounds. Although appearing "consumptive," they claimed she could exert the force of about "one horsepower. The article should have been titled, "The Fantasy of a Woman," for Mattie tells her childhood story, much embellished. "Her parents died when she was 7 years old, and she was adopted by people who were not her relatives. How long she has had the power she does not know, but she discovered it when 9 years old. The discovery was made on the playground, where she found she could shove all the children of the school around the yard at will." Here it was claimed that Mattie had made over $100,000 since her first show in Chicago "four or five years ago." Since Mattie did not go to school as a child and was never adopted out of her family, it is quite conceivable that she simply dreamed up the story that she had "laid up" a hundred thousand dollars.

While Mattie did not deny that she was "under the influence of spirits" as others had claimed, "she was by no means convinced of it." She had never encountered any of the unexplained flying objects or "rappings" from unseen forces such as those Lulu Hurst and Annie Abbott claimed to have experienced. She had "never seen any apparitions or materializations." However, "she has the power of healing by the laying on of hands, but uses it sparingly, as she believes when she heals a disease she takes it on herself."

The article explained (again) how Mattie was able to lift men and twist sticks as had been thoroughly outlined before, but now there were two new feats not earlier described.

One of these was "The Balancing Test" where Mattie stood facing a gentleman holding a stick. Mattie stood on one foot, holding up one hand to resist the end of the stick. No matter how hard the man pushed on the stick, he could not make Mattie lose her balance.

The second newly depicted feat was of Mattie holding a chair in such a way that two men could not force it to the ground. All matter of people tested her. There were even doctors prodding, measuring, and taking notes and scientists attempting to prove electricity or magnetism as the force behind her abilities. The least pleasant were members of the "committee" of men with whom she demonstrated her strength. Some became so angry and frustrated that they struck her!

✐

Mattie Price married Louis Barella on 10 January 1894 in Chicago, Illinois. The marriage license states both were from "Chattoga, Tennessee." There is no such place, so either the clerk of court couldn't spell Chattanooga or the newlyweds made it up. Mattie was good at storytelling and getting better it seems. Did she ever secure a legal divorce from Samuel Wise or W. W. White?

Courtesy of the Cook County Clerk's Office, Chicago, IL

Although there were lots of "Louis Barella" immigrants of about Mattie's age in the United States at the time, most were ordinary workingmen with wives and children and were absolutely not any part of Mattie Lee Price's life. However, there were a few flashes of the possible real Louis Barella sprinkled about in newspapers that were probably written about Mattie's new heartthrob.

July 6, 1890 the *Sunday Herald* in Boston, Massachusetts, printed an advertisement for Austin and Stone's Museum on Tremont Row, Scollay Square. "Barella, The Man of Mystery" was one of the featured acts for the following day. (p. 11, col. 7). He was there with "La Selle, the queen of the aquarium" and her friend, "Amphibro, the aquatic marvel."

Two months later and 225 miles southwest of Boston, a little girl of seventeen eloped with twenty-three-year-old "Prof. Barella," a magician who was working at the museum in Newark, New Jersey. Her parents were totally taken aback and word was sent out to police departments far and wide to try to find the wayward girl. (The *New Haven Register* (New Haven, Connecticut), 4 Sep 1890, v. XLVIII, issue 210, p. 4). The girl, who was really only sixteen, telegraphed her father soon after her elopement and asked to come home since her "dreams" of happiness were over and she "didn't want anything to do with him," the fire-eater, anymore. (The *New York Herald* (New York, New York), 19 Sep 1890, issue 262, p. 5).

Twenty-two-year-old Mattie Lee Price had been in Buffalo, New York, at Robinson's Musee on September 14, 1891. On the bill with her was "Barnello, the fire eater, who eats, drinks, and inhales fire. He is a real wonder." (The *Buffalo Morning Express*, 14 September 1891, p. 5, col. 6). It doesn't take much of a leap to conclude that "Barnello" was a simply a misspelling of "Barella," who was likely the same man who eloped with the sixteen-year-old girl the year before. How many fire-eaters with such a similar name could there have been? Might this have been when and where the lovebirds first met?

The *Chicago Inter Ocean* placed "Barella the Magician" at the Globe Dime Museum ten months later on 31 July 1892. (The *Daily Inter Ocean*, 31 July 1892, p. 20, col. 4). We have no information as to Mattie's whereabouts at the time.

"The Hamlin-Barella European Novelty Company" was set to begin at Kohl & Middleton's in Cincinnati the week of 11 September 1892. Apparently they walked on knives with bare feet, and this appearance was their first, ever, anywhere. (The *Cincinnati Enquirer*, 11 Sep 1892, p. 11, col. 4). Two days later, the act was given rave reviews in the *Cincinnati Enquirer* in an advertisement likely paid for by the museum. The knife walkers were sensational and Barella did a great magic act. (The *Cincinnati Enquirer*, 13 Sep 1892, p. 6, col. 6). On 18 September, Hamlin-Barella and company were still in Cincinnati at Kohl & Middleton's. On the same bill was "Ogalalla, the fire-eating Indian Chief." Was this Barella doubling his income by being both a "magician" and a "fire eater" at the museum? Mattie worked at the same museum one month after Barella.

The next Barella newspaper tidbit was on 22 February 1893 in Cincinnati. It was curious. A man by the name of George R. Martin left a boarding house without paying. "He claimed to represent Allen & Barella, of this city." However, Martin was a partner, not just an agent. "George A. Allen, of Cleveland, and Lewis Barella, of Chicago, came here sometime ago as agents of Steece Store Stool Company and rented desk-room in the office of R. M. McLinn, of the Rental Company, in the Bacon Building, Sixth and Walnut streets." George Martin also borrowed $18 from McLinn (the landlord), and when asked to repay the money, he refused. McLinn planned to sue for the return of the money, but Martin, Allen, and Barella skipped town without repaying the $18 loan or the $8 they owned for the desk space they had rented. Allegedly, the trio had "beaten several people in the city also." They were con men. (The *Cincinnati Enquirer*, 22 Feb 1893, p. 8, col. 4). We have no idea where Mattie Lee Price was at that time.

We cannot prove one way or another if the Barella mentioned in these articles was the same Barella who married Mattie Lee Price on 10 January of 1894, but it probably was. All of the other right-aged Barella gentlemen who turned up during research seemed to be stabile family men. The magician, fire-eating Barella did not seem to be either successful or honest, if the newspapers are to be believed.

Mattie was ready to start her act at Frank Hall's Casino, but the painted canvas that served as a curtain had not gone up yet. Mr. Hall, in an attempt to hype Mattie's act announced, "I'll give $1,000—yes $5,000" to anyone who could explain how 'The Mysterious Gaza' accomplished her feats." To his horror, a short, stout little English engineer with a "broad forehead and neatly trimmed beard," accepted the challenge. The Englishman's name was the T. H. Brigg and he had, for some time, been trying to convince the masses about the wisdom of using his theories with regard to horses and hauling. Apparently, the way things were "always done," not only wore down the horses, but was highly inefficient. Brigg knew how to haul more load with less wear and tear on the horseflesh. Brigg wanted to prove his theories on Mattie, on the stage, at that very moment. Frank Hall, the owner declared that it was not a good time. Such a demonstration would disrupt the show. He said the people had come to see Mattie, not Mr. Brigg.

The audience went a little confrontational and insisted that Brigg be given a chance to win the $5,000. They smelled blood. Mr. Hall, facing a losing situation, gave the signal to have the canvas raised so the act could begin. Mattie and her manager were already waiting on the stage. The "committee of twelve" men who were to interact with "Gaza" took their places. They had been previously selected. Mr. Brigg, not chosen as one of the committee, "climbed down out of his box and started up the steps leading from the orchestra to the stage."

He was not going to let it go. Mr. Hall grabbed at him to stop him, but Mr. Brigg was a strong little man. The theater attaché appeared just then and assisted Mr. Hall until Brigg was finally subdued. The audience became unruly in reaction to the struggle. "The scene ended by a man in plain clothes climbing over the excited throng and going through the pantomime of showing a star." Everyone calmed down. Brigg and Hall returned to their respective places and Mattie began demonstrating "her usual feats." Mr. Brigg yelled "Tommy rot!" and "bosh!" from his box during the act and Mr. Hall, holding his steam during Mattie's performance, boiled over the moment the canvas went down.

Mr. Hall grabbed Mr. Brigg in anger and a "muscular young man weighting fully 200 pounds, who had served on the committee, sprang over the railing with an exclamation of wrath, tearing off his coat as he went. He thrust an enormous fist under Mr. Hall's nose and in loud and emphatic language informed him that the gentleman had paid for his seat and he was behaving, and that he was not going to be imposed upon while the speaker was around." Mr. Brigg and the young man "exchanged cards," and the engineer gleefully began dealing out his cards to a throng of outstretched hands.

Most of the audience was shouting opinions and taunting Mr. Hall, whom they felt had broken his promise of $5,000 to anyone who could prove how Mattie did her act. Suddenly, the house lights were extinguished and the audience "groped its way out" of the theater. (*Chicago Daily Tribune*, 11 Jan 1894, p. 1, col. 5–6).

Mr. Brigg was not finished. He would be listened to that day. He called a couple of "muscular colored porters employed at the Leland, where he is staying. When the porters arrived Mr. Brigg took the role of Gaza. It is true he does not look the part, for he is distinctly stout, while Gaza is spirituelle, but he performed all of her feats." Brigg provided diagrams to the *Chicago Daily Tribune* showing precisely how "Gaza has pulled the wool over people's eyes in England and in America." While Brigg was most certainly intent upon trumpeting his brilliant engineering knowledge of physics, he did so in such a way as to be quite demeaning to Miss Mattie Lee Price. The *Tribune's* article was titled, "Gaza's Gauzy Tricks." In the article Brigg submitted drawings to explain how Mattie did her act.

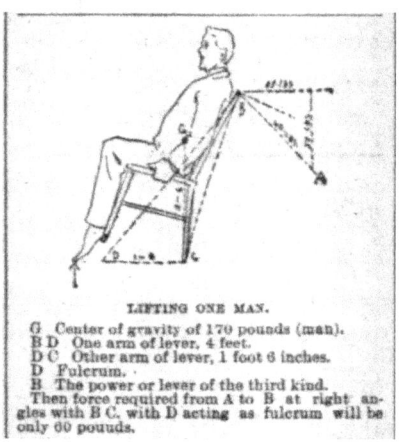

LIFTING ONE MAN.

G   Center of gravity of 170 pounds (man).
B D   One arm of lever, 4 feet.
D C   Other arm of lever, 1 foot 6 inches.
D   Fulcrum.
B   The power or lever of the third kind.
 Then force required from A to B at right angles with B C, with D acting as fulcrum will be only 60 pounds.

Chicago Tribune, Newspapers.com ~ with permission

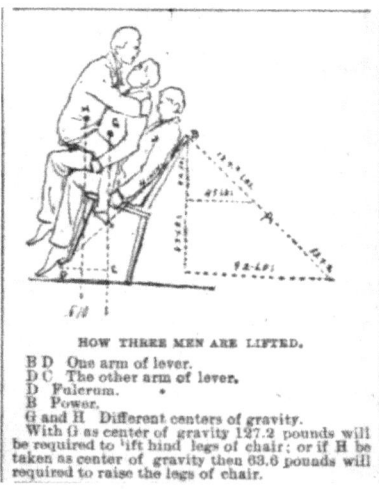

HOW THREE MEN ARE LIFTED.

B D   One arm of lever.
D C   The other arm of lever.
D   Fulcrum.
B   Power.
G and H   Different centers of gravity.
 With G as center of gravity 127.2 pounds will be required to 'ift hind legs of chair; or if H be taken as center of gravity then 63.6 pounds will required to raise the legs of chair.

Chicago Tribune, Newspapers.com ~ with permission

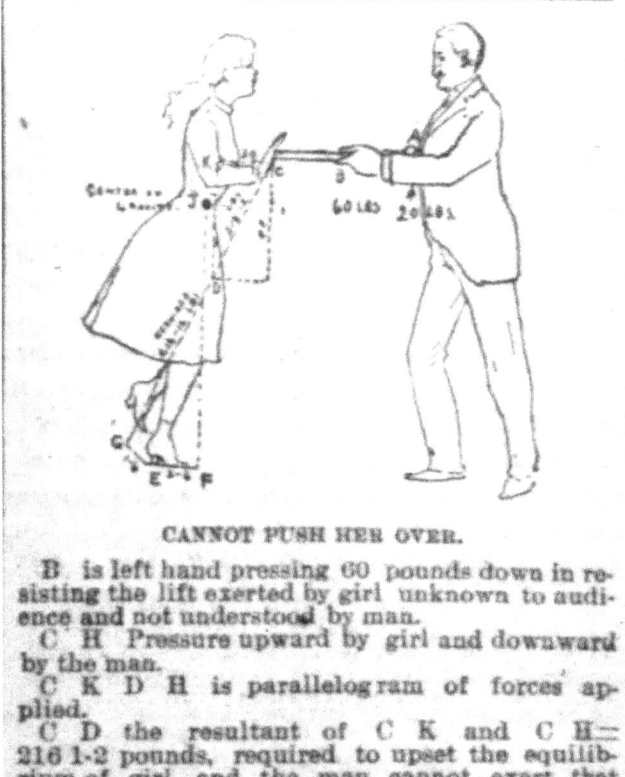

**CANNOT PUSH HER OVER.**

B is left hand pressing 60 pounds down in resisting the lift exerted by girl unknown to audience and not understood by man.

C H Pressure upward by girl and downward by the man.

C K D H is parallelogram of forces applied.

C D the resultant of C K and C H = 216 1-2 pounds, required to upset the equilibrium of girl, and the man cannot exert that force under those conditions.

E F is one arm of bent lever upon which her natural weight (90 pounds) is acting together, with the added weight C H, or 40 pounds, equaling 130 pounds.

C E is short arm of bent lever determined by C D, at the extremity of which the resultant of the man's thrust is effected.

Regardless of how brutally Brigg trampled on Mattie's reputation, his vociferous declarations boosted attendance at Frank Hall's Casino. Hall advertised that he had convinced the Mysterious Gaza to cancel her previously scheduled appearances elsewhere and to extend her stay at his theater "at a largely increased salary." Apparently there really is no such thing as "bad press."

On 24 January 1894, the *Chicago Tribune* (p. 8, col. 5). announced that Frank Hall was going to take up T. H. Brigg's challenge "of $1,000" to explain Mattie's act. Evidently, the $5,000 was shrunk back to the smaller number.

The Inter-Ocean, Newspapers.com ~ with permission

The challenge would take place on "Saturday evening, Feb. 24." The prices seem to have increased to 15 cents for the cheapest seats, and the best seats, all the way to $1.00. Brigg promised that, "Captain Hennesy of the Fire Brigade (who by reason of a broken leg is unable to walk without assistance) will by an application of the… forces, be enabled to discard his crutches, and will haul a heavily laden wagon on the stage" Gaza herself promised twelve new tests (feats) would be demonstrated to the 2,900 people expected to fill the theater for the contest. Brigg submitted yet more diagrams of his theories to the newspapers. (*The Inter Ocean* (Chicago, Illinois), 18 Feb 1894, p. 16, col. 7).

A committee was selected to appear on stage with Mattie the night of the challenge, 23 February 1894. The men listed were, "John G. Shortall, President of the Illinois Humany Society; Fire Marshal Swenie, Assistant Fire Marshal Petrie, Drs. R.J. Withers, A.H.Baker, Joseph Hughes, President, Treasurer, and Secretary of the Chicago Veterinary College: Dr. McKillop, No. 1639 Wabash avenue; J.S. Cooper, contractor, No. 450 Indiana street; H.D.Staver of Staver, Abbott & Co., No 385 Wabash avenue; F. H. McAdoo, No 385 Wabash avenue; W. J. Clizbe, Manager Milburn Wagon company." (*Chicago Tribune*, 24 Feb 1894, p. 6, col. 3).

Brigg was enjoying the notoriety the challenge afforded him. Long articles about him and his mathematical, scientific theories about leverage and "economic power" appeared in Chicago newspapers. The whole escapade would become not only national but international news. Brigg claimed that, "forces used by "Gaza" are not hypnotic, but are practical applications of the natural powers owned by all animals alike, and tonight will endeavor to scientifically prove his theories." (One is reminded of a cock rooster crowing about his amazing insight and power over the lesser hen). Brigg wanted to convince the public that horses could be more scientifically harnessed so as to provide better leverage. This would improve a horse's overall ability to move loads and better "economize" its strength. Perhaps, from his point of view, Mattie was simply a way to transport his ideas forward. To some scientists, the furthering of "facts and truth" is far more important than preserving the dignity of mere "people." Briggs reveled in the attention. Since Mattie had never attended school but did her act intuitively, she was probably just as curious as everyone else as to the principles that lay behind her ability to move and resist objects. The evening came and the house was packed.

"To Conserve Forces. T.H. Brigg uses Gaza to Illustrate His Principles," led the article on page 5 of the *Chicago Tribune* on the twenty-fifth. "What a horse can do when it is hitched to a vehicle, as to the custom at present, and what it can do when hitched as it should be, with a proper understanding of natural laws, was shown by T. H. Brigg at Central Music Hall last night. It was shown that horses were compelled to work at great disadvantage, but that it is entirely practicable to give them at all times a mechanical advantage over their load."

Brigg had Mattie join him on the stage and demonstrate her feats of strength. "Then by stereopticon views and practical experiments he explained the forces exerted, and explained that they were identical with the forces exerted by horses."

"When Mr. Brigg began his explanations Hall interrupted him with a continuation of his harangue, but the audience shut him off with hoots and hisses." The exchange went on for about ten minutes when finally Hall gave up and let Brigg continue. Brigg went through modifications of Mattie's feats and was able to show the audience that, in all practicality, anyone could do it. Brigg continued to lecture the audience upon the benefits of properly harnessing a horse using the same principles he had demonstrated and ended with, "Don't forget the profit; for it is upon this rock that I must build my hope of bettering the condition and usefulness of the poor horse."

Brigg was accused of following Mattie's act all the way from London a year and a half earlier. In a public statement in the *Chicago Daily Inter Ocean*, he strongly denied the accusation, and declared he had only seen Gaza some five weeks prior in Chicago. "My conduct at the Casino and my determination to urge on the contest at any cost was on behalf of the horse and not for either Mr. Hall or his money." (*Daily Inter Ocean*, 1 March 1894, p. 7, col. 1). One senses the slightest hint of remorse for the insensitivity shown Mattie but with no apology for the righteous bullheadedness with which he delivered his ideas.

Mattie, dressed in an exotic costume, was again photographed in the famous Eisenmann studio in New York. We assume this costume was in line with her "Gaza" stage name.

Courtesy of the Warren A Raymond Collection

# — Chapter Thirteen —

"WONDERFUL GAZA" WAS SLATED TO begin showing at H. R. Jacob's Clark Street Theater in mid-March 1894. There hadn't even been a pause for Mattie after the Brigg affair at Hall's Casino.

The *Winnipeg Tribune* (Winnipeg, Manitoba, Canada, 10 March 1894, p. 6) reported "Annie Abbott, the little magnet is doing one night stands now, and to poor business lately." Abbott was doing better in April according to the *Springfield Leader* in Missouri. They said, "She is really a wonder."

Also in March, the *Leeds Times* (England, 31 March 1894, p. 5, col. 1). reported on the Brigg affair at Frank Hall's Casino. Brigg, an Englishman, was portrayed as a homegrown hero and as having, "English obstinacy and scientific knowledge of force." They wrote that

Brigg was victorious and Gaza was defeated and that Hall "kept his 1,000 dollars" while "Gaza and her very tall, very dark lecturer, were crest-fallen and very angry." Mattie's husband, Barella, was obviously very tall and very dark. Was he Italian? It is doubtful that Mattie lost her temper that night. Never in ten years of newspaper articles (both complimentary and disparaging) was there ever mention of her being angry or even upset.

The Walter L. Main Circus was on the road again April of 1894. The devastated circus had been rebuilt after the train wreck and tragedy at Tyrone, Pennsylvania, on 30 May 1893. The show was "being transported… to Lewiston, via the Tyrone Clearfield branch of the Pennsylvania railroad." The 1893 wreck killed five men and injured twelve. "William Jenks, keeper, had his left knee cap bitten off by a lion." As of May 31, 1893, there were still many circus animals running loose including a lion, a tiger, and a panther. "One tiger entered the yard of Alfred Thomas, a farmer, when his wife was about to milk their two cows. The tiger, a Bengal beast, leaped on one of the cows and killed it. Forty-eight horses were killed, including the trained ring horses." All in all, sixteen cages of animals had escaped; all but the three big cats were captured by the next day. Killed in the train wreck were "William Henry, brakeman, Tyrone; Grank Brain, Indianapolis, Ind; William Murperly, East Liberty, Pa; John Stayer, Houtzdale, Pa; Lonie Chaplain, Rochester, N.Y. The injured were taken to the hospital in Altoons." (The *Evening Herald* (Shenandoah, Pennsylvania), 31 May, 1893, p. 1, col. 5).

Mattie Lee Price, working as "Gaza," joined the Walter L. Main Circus around 18 May 1894. Gaza first appeared in an advertisement for the Elkhart, Indiana, circus stop scheduled for the twenty-first. (The

*Elkhart Daily Review*, 18 May 1894, p. 4, col. 5). While she was not actually listed in every Walter Main's Circus advertisement, she was evident in Cleveland in late May and early June. The circus advertised a three-ring circus, hippodrome, a menagerie, and the "only horses on earth trained to play base ball." It was no small circus indeed, as the claim was that one thousand men and horses were employed. The show was held under a "waterproof tent." "Gaza, the strong woman, live rooster orchestra… and streets of Cairo reproduced." (The "streets of Cairo" referred to the 1893 World Columbian Fair, presumably). And although it was unheard of to promote a sideshow act to the center ring, that is exactly what happened to Mattie. Walter L. Main gave her a starring role in his 1894 circus and a big, beautiful lithograph poster was produced to promote her. The advertisement illustrates and describes six of her different feats of strength and declares, "The Magnetic Wonder a Human Magnet of Strength and Weight the phenomenon of the 19th century, lifting hundreds of pounds of dead weight by just placing her hands on it, twisting bars of iron, resisting as much force as can push on a 12 foot pole by simply placing her hands at one end. It cannot be justly pictured, no words adequate to describe it."

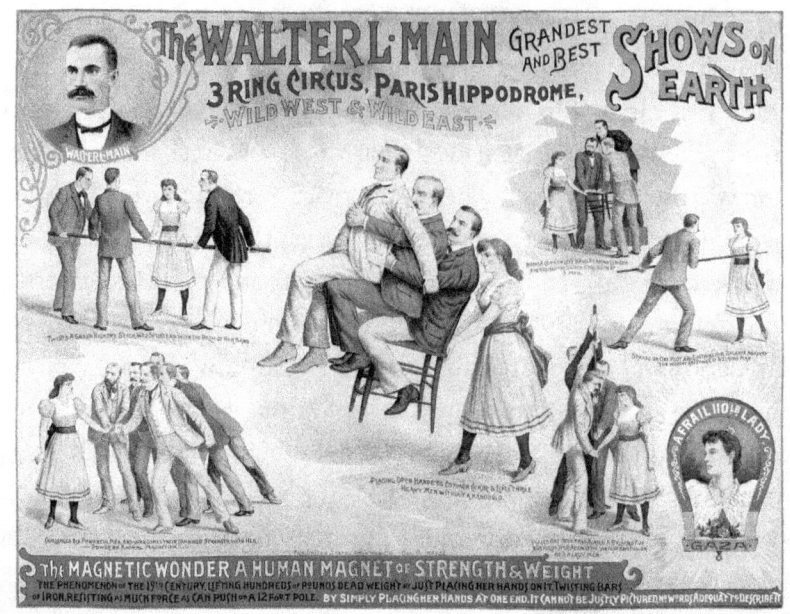

Courtesy of the Ken Harck circus collection

Back in Chicago, the "White City" at the Columbian World Fair grounds was almost completely destroyed in a fire they believed was caused by an incendiary. "The buildings saved...the Horticultural Building, the Woman's Building, the Art Palace, the Machinery Building and the United States Building."

The Walter L. Main Circus stopped by a place called a "Hygienic Institute" (11 August) in White Plains, New York. It was there that stressed-out politicians and the like could seek calm and quiet and recover from their tension-filled lives. They were given meat three times a day, although it was limited. All were to be up by 6:00 a.m. and to bed by 9:00 p.m. "There are billiard and pool tables for recreation, and music, which, when ladies are with their husbands, makes the evening very enjoyable." The Walter L. Main Circus arrived and the quiet peacefulness was set-aside for the day. "They all hugely enjoyed the sight of a lion riding on the back of a horse, the hippodrome races and the magnetic feats of 'Mlle. Gaza.'"

The Walter L. Main circus train suffered a nondamaging collision in Flushing, New York, on 14 August. "One section, with the engine, was on a side-track in charge of Conductor McKeever. The other section was loading up with animals just beyond the tunnel at Murray Hill. From Murray Hill to Flushing is a downgrade, and the section, instead of being driven by an engine, was allowed to run down of its own momentum. A single brakeman was guiding the cars. Coming into Flushing an attempt to make a flying switch caused the two sections to crash together." While nothing was damaged and no one hurt, one can only imagine the cold finger of fear that ran down the spines of the veteran circus men; it was just fifteen months since the horrible accident in Tyrone, Pennsylvania. ("Lions and Tigers Roared," Sporting Extra *Evening World*, 14 Aug 1894, p. 3, col. 3).

Gaza was mentioned in a Walter L. Main's advertisement for Accomac, Virginia, in late September 1894. (The *Peninsula Enterprise*, 29 Sept 1894, p. 2, col. 4). Now she was "Gaza, the Electric Wonder."

The Walter L. Main's Circus entertained Columbia, South Carolina, in late September. They boasted over five hundred horses and gave some highlights of the coming attraction: "Horseback riding lion, two-headed cow, Gaza, the magnetic girl, performing troupe of Arabian horses, rooster orchestra, troupes of Japs and Arabs, twenty-one horses driven by one man, etc." (The State, (Columbia, South Carolina), 23 Oct 1894, p. 3).

And at long last, Mattie was back in Georgia. On 16 November 1894, the Walter L. Main Show put on a circus in Thomasville with, among others, the "only living American-Born Monkeys, Gaza the Electric Wonder, Highly Educated Elephants…and Den of Baby

Lions born July 4, 1894." This was the only time we ever found Mattie back in Georgia.

The estimated number of stops that the Walter L. Main Circus made that year was about 146 and that was before the "Grand Southern Tour," which included South Carolina and Georgia (www.circushistory.org/Routes/WalterMain1928.htm#1894).

Circus life was grueling. The performers did their shows, packed everything onto a train, traveled to the next showplace, unloaded everything, did their shows and repeated—almost every single day for six months. Children sometimes traveled with their parents, but more often than not performers left their children with relatives or acquaintances and the children only reunited with their nomadic parents after the end of the circus season. There was nothing published to indicate where Mattie's children stayed. Jenny was eight and Charles was six in 1894.

# — Chapter Fourteen —

Gaza was scheduled for "Victor's High Class Vaudeville Combination" in Cincinnati, Ohio in mid-December. (The *Cincinnati Post*, 15 Dec 1894, p. 2, col. 1). She was further advertised to appear at Victor's the twenty-second through the twenty-sixth of January.

On 20 February 1895, a woman listed as "Miss M. Price, Seamstress" arrived alone in New York from Liverpool, England. She was twenty-seven, Mattie's age. It might have been her. She rarely listed her marital status as anything but single, and she never listed her correct occupation. She seemed to enjoy being an enigma.

Mattie was in Midway, Kentucky, on 27 March at the Collins Opera House. (The *New York Daily Mirror*, 6 April 1895, p. 6, col. 1).

The 1895, Barnum and Bailey Circus route began in Madison Square Gardens, March 28, 1895. Mattie must have joined them soon after her Kentucky show, for we find her nowhere else at the time.

We find Mattie listed as part of the "Concert Company" in the 1895 circus route book. The "concert" of a circus was essentially the after-the-show show in which musicians and other talented members of the "Concert Company" entertained lingering circus guests. There was usually a separate charge for this show. That year Maud Rosselle (serio comic), Johnson & Williamson (Black Face Team), Jessie Millar (Solo Cornetist), Wade and Hastings (Sketch Artists), Tambourine McCarty (Tambourine Manipulator), Larry & Hart (Eccentric Song and Dance), and Millie Lee Price (Gaza) formed the "Concert Company." Obviously Mattie's name was misspelled, but her advertisement on page 95 of the same official route book got it right.

Barnum and Bailey Route Book 1895

One should note the particularly large and fluffy sleeves on Mattie's dress in the route book advertisement. They appear enormous, cumbersome, and impractical, to say the least. Fabric of those days wrinkled miserably and it must have been a full-time job to keep them beautifully inflated. "The Balloon Sleeves from a Man's Point of View," was the title of an article in Lima News in Ohio regarding the puffy apparel. "You really can't get near a girl nowadays." His lady friend required him to stay his distance and avoid "crushing my sleeves out of shape." (The *Lima New* (Lima Ohio), 12 June 1895, p. 3). Balloon sleeves were also extremely dangerous. Two women lost their lives in Chicago because of them. A nineteen-year-old girl caught her sleeves in the gas flame and began to burn. When her mother attempted to save her, she was burned as well. Miss Helena Riggs and her mother, Emma Riggs, forty-seven, lost their lives to fashion's folly. (The *Chicago Tribune*, 13 September 1895, p. 1, col. 5).

The regular Barnum & Bailey 1895 "Curiosities and Performers" were listed as Annie Jones (Bearded Lady), Lulu La Toska (Snake Enchantress, M'lle Lulu (Lady Magician), Jo-Jo (Dog Face Boy), Fred Warner, (Blue Man), Waino and Plutano (Wild Men of Borneo), Chas. B. Tripp (Armless Phenomenon), James Wilson (Expansionist), John Orsona (Wire Haired Man), Zip (Barnum's "What is it?"), Paul Schweigerling, and John Walton (Marionettes).

The 1895 circus was bigger and better than ever before and included "The Grand Water Carnival." "Louis Golden's headlong dive of sixty-three feet into seven feet of water at 70 degrees is thrilling enough, but his limit—ninety feet—cannot be tested in Madison Square Gardens. The room is not high enough." There was "logrolling" and a comic act that accompanied it in which "the band, tramps, policemen, picnic parties, and anglers" were involuntarily immersed. "Monte Cristo is remembered, when he, tied up in a sack, is dropped into the water to extricate himself and to air as speedily as he may." There were clowns, horse racers, foreign peoples ("Cave dwellers to the Samoan") and all sorts of acrobats. ("All Like the Big Circus," The *New York Times*, 17 April 1895, p. 16, col. 2).

Courtesy of the Library of Congress

On 19 April, George Dunbar, a trapeze artist "leaped from his bar, missed catching his brother's hands and fell into the net 40 feet below, which went down with a crash, landing him on the ground." His shoulder was dislocated; He broke ribs, and suffered internal injuries. Although badly hurt, he did not die of his injuries. ("Fell From Trapeze," the *Trenton Evening Times* (Trenton, New Jersey), 19 April 1895, p. 2).

A reporter of the *New York Times* interviewed a circus woman by the name of Mrs. Wentworth. She described circus life as being sometimes difficult for a woman, but a lot of idle time was passed doing "fancy work." Outside of the circus, the performers did have homes to decorate even if they were traveling a lot. It was also likely that some of the circus performers spent their spare time styling and perfecting their own costumes. Even though Mrs. White, wife of the lion tamer was responsible for all the "regular" performer's attire, sideshow and concert performers were not her concern. Mattie provided her own costumes, while the monkeys, and elephants, did not.

Mrs. Wentworth said that married couples had the bottom bunks on the circus train while singles had the top. Since one was allowed to use the same bunk all of the time, these areas were often decorated to suit the user. At first she thought it difficult to put up with the meandering circus life, but she soon became accustomed to falling asleep in one city and waking up in another and thought it quite exciting.

The *Jersey Journal* was duly impressed with the Barnum & Bailey Circus in May. Performances given under the big circus tent in Oakland Park were full to capacity. "The fakirs on the outside of the show who dispensed red lemonade and peanuts were fully persuaded that the circus was one of the greatest and most beneficent institutions on the globe, for they can make more money and more people sick when the circus is in town than at any other time." There was good reason the lemonade might make people sick. To quote an old circus man who started working in the circus in the 1860s, George Conklin, "The fact that lemonade of a pink color would be more popular and sell faster than the ordinary variety was discovered quite accidentally in 1857 by my brother Pete." The origin of the "pink" in lemonade, according to Mr. Conklin, was the result of a shortage of water.

Fannie Jamieson, one of the bareback riders, had just finished wringing out a pair of pink tights. The color had run and left the water a deep pink. Without giving any explanation or stopping to answer her questions, Pete grabbed the tub of pink water and ran. It took only a minute to throw in some of the tartaric acid and the pieces of the "property" lemon, and then he began to call out, "Come quickly, buy some fine strawberry lemonade."That day his sales doubled and from then on, no first-class circus was without pink lemonade." Mr. Conklin gave up the secret ingredients for the lemonade, too. "The recipe for circus lemonade has not changed from that day…A tub of water—with no particular squeamishness regarding its source—tartaric acid, some sugar, enough aniline dye to give it a rich pink, and for the finish some thin slices of lemon. The slices of lemon are known as "floaters," and any which are left in the tub at the close of day's business, together with those which have come back in the glasses, are carefully saved over for the next day's use. (*The Ways of the Circus: Being the Memories and Adventures of George Conklin, Tamer of Lions*, set down by Harvey W. Root, Harper & Brothers Publishers, New York and London, 1921, p. 230, Google eBook).

The sideshows did good business at Oakland Park in early May, but the reporter felt the concert that followed was not worth the ten cents for the musical show. It all went well, however "and nobody found fault." (*Jersey Journal* (New Jersey, Jersey City), 7 May 1895, p. 5, col. 2).

In Decatur, Illinois, the show ran into another snag. "Doctors Suspected Smallpox." Apparently two of the Indian women in the "Barnum and Bailey Ethnological Congress"fell ill. A member of "the board of health" thought they had smallpox. They had a plethora of doctors examine the women, but no one could clearly diagnose the problem. The whole circus was in danger of being quarantined for the rest of the season. "One doctor finally declared the disease to be rothien, or German fever."The show was allowed to continue on to

Bloomington, but the Indian women stayed back in the sanitarium. (The *Chicago Inter Ocean*, 4 June 1895, p. 2, col. 2).

Buffalo Bill Cody and the manager of the Barnum & Bailey's Circus had petitioned Secretary of the Interior Hoke for permission to employ Indians in their shows and that permission had been granted in January 1895. (The *San Francisco Chronicle*, 25 Jan 1895, p. 4, col. 6).

One can imagine watching the circus materializing at dawn in the city of Cleveland on 1 July 1895. The weather had been ninety degrees the day before, but showers and a light, northerly, wind were predicted for that day. The crew arrived, "tape measure in hand," and laid out where all the tents should be. There were 208 side poles and 5 center poles for the big tent. Then there were tents for dressing rooms, wardrobe, sideshow freaks' dressing room, and six or so tents for maintenance, blacksmith, and what not. "Three large cook wagons… each weighing twenty tons, and drawn by six horses" arrived. The kitchen tent was not yet erected, but three butchers commenced butchering the beef, mutton, and pork. There would be eight hundred hungry diners within two hours and breakfast preparations were well underway. Reporters had been invited to dine with the circus and enjoyed a special program. Steak with mushrooms, French peas, cold meats, ham and eggs, loin of pork, prime ribs of beef, tea, and coffee were served. They sat on chairs with no backs and ate. The whole operation was efficient and quick, and in no time the circus was fully erected and ready for the show. ("The Circus," The *Plain Dealer* (Cleveland, Ohio), 1 July 1895, p. 8, col. 1–2 and p. 1, col. 6).

There were thieves and con men both within the circus and following it. Scotty's Gang of Chicago had been following the Barnum & Bailey and they were arrested on 29 June in Findlay, Ohio. Jimmy Cain was the thief, and he picked the pocket of Mrs. Jacob Thompson taking $35. "Scotty was also arrested while engaged in robbing a lady, and thirty-one others of his gang are locked up on suspicion."

("Scotty's Gang in Jail," The *Inter Ocean* (Chicago, Illinois), 30 June 1895, p. 4, col. 2).

Ottawa, Ontario, Canada, welcomed the circus in late July. "The new feature of the parade was the representation of national troops of the world. The characters were all well taken except that of the Irishman that they tried to make a Chinese Dragoon of. You can't make a Chinaman out of an Irishman. They ain't built on the same lines." The circus had come from Montreal, taking three trains consisting of sixty cars. The Ottawa Journal reporter related the "Big Feed Bill" for the circus animals. There were "Twelve tons of hay… also four loads of straw for bedding and fifty bushels of oats as well as large quantities of vegetables…" and about 1,400 pounds of meat for the lions and other animals. " Slattery and Terrance supplied 800 lbs. of beef, pork, lamb and other meats for the feeding of the people connected with the circus." He counts the total number of folks in the circus at three hundred, sixty-two of whom were cooks and waiters. The reporter also suggested, tongue in cheek, that if you were an adult, it was advantages to "have a kid" as a grown-up excuse to visit the circus. (*Ottawa Journal* (Ontario, Canada), 24 July 1895, p. 1).

Chicago had looked forward to hosting the 1895 Barnum & Bailey Circus at its new coliseum building being constructed on the old site of the "Buffalo Bill Wild West Show," adjacent to the World Columbian Exposition in Jackson Park. The building had enormous dimensions, and the builders had hastened to get it done in time for the circus to inaugurate the structure. The circus (and the concert with Mattie Lee Price) was scheduled to be in Chicago September 2 through 14. Unfortunately, the iron roof of the gigantic building collapsed on 21 August. Not only could Chicago not celebrate the grand opening of the building, which cost at least $225,000, but the great Barnum & Bailey Circus was left without a location to set up its tents. (The *Evansville Courier* (Indiana), 22 Aug 1895, p. 1, col.

3). Of this incident, the official route book relates, "Mr. Bailey upon whom the mantle of the illustrious Barnum has fallen, has undoubtedly discovered that a collapse is just as good as a fire for advertising purposes." Indeed, they did wonderful business in Chicago.

The circus would eventually set up at 25th Street and South Park Avenue for six days and then move to "the old West side baseball grounds at Harrison and Loomis streets six day following." Bailey would deliver two separate circus parades! Lucky Chicago! (The *Daily Inter Ocean*, 27 August 1895, p. 8).

And so it was that the circus finally arrived in Chicago at 3:30 in the morning on Sunday, 1 September 1895, in "four of the oddest looking trains that ever entered the city." The cars were especially constructed and owned by the circus. One could only glimpse the "gaudily painted wagons" that were covered by canvases, but when 'the herd of twenty-four elephants' unloaded just after 4 am, they were hard to miss. They were not only big, they were loud, and 'their loud trumpetings expressed their joy at being liberated from the cars.'" Mr. Bailey did not like working on Sundays more "than is absolutely necessary." (The *Daily Inter Ocean* (Chicago, Illinois), 1 September 1895, p. 8, col. 2).

There was a fire in a barn on 8 September, ignited by a careless smoker. Firemen put it out and there was little damage. (*Daily Inter Ocean*, 9 September 1895, p. 8, col. 6).

For Mattie, Chicago was home. Her permanent address, which was printed on her advertisement in the 1895 route book, was listed as 1559 S. State Street, Chicago, Illinois. The city directory for 1895 lists a saloon owned by Jacob Aronson at that address in downtown Chicago. The name Aronson would show up again in Mattie's life a little farther down the road. Was this a boarding house as well as a saloon? Were her children living there? Since she was a part of the concert program that performed after the main circus, certainly she had time during the day to be with them, if they were in Chicago.

The circus left Chicago and continued onward, showing in Milwaukee, Madison, Freeport, Dixon, Clinton, Davenport, Galesburg, and Quincy, Illinois. Everything went well until Burlington, Iowa. The official route book says it best.

> Wednesday, Sept. 25. Lot, West Hill. Business fair. Everybody with the show will have cause to remember Burlington, as the worst cyclone that the Barnum Show has ever met with occurred here today. All day the weather was threatening and a pretty stiff wind was blowing; the afternoon show was cut in consequence of the approach of a severe storm, which reached us with terrific force about five o'clock in the afternoon, when the wind commenced to blow a perfect hurricane, striking our tents with terrific force. After standing it for a few minutes the big top, horse tents and the cookhouse succumbed to the wind and were blown down. The Side-show, Menagerie, dressing-room and one horse-tent remained standing, though terribly torn. The big top was so badly destroyed it was impossible to repair it. During all this the rain poured down in torrents, flooding the lot and compelling the men who were clearing up the wreckage to walk in water knee-deep. The ticket sellers, candy butchers, and in fact, everybody, deserve great credit for the way they worked clearing up the wreck.
>
> Mr. Bailey telegraphed "Mr. Pig" in Bridgeport, Connecticut, and requested last year's tent be delivered. (*The Barnum & Bailey Official Route Book Season of 1895*, published by George E. Hardy. P. 73, col 1).

The enormously successful show continued on through Wyoming, Colorado, Texas, and Louisiana where Mr. Louis Barella, Mattie's manager and husband made the papers. In the "First Recorder's Court, Recorder E.S. Whitiker presiding," Barella was fined for "disturbing the peace and insult and abuse." He could choose between sixty days in jail or a $50 fine. The circus itself was also under threat of lawsuit. "Jos. N. Wolfson, attorney for Henry C. Mahan, yesterday sued Barnum & Bailey proprietors of the big circus for $25,000 damages from injuries sustained at the circus on Monday night. Mahan claims to have been abused, beaten and injured by the employees of the circus." Was Mahan's abuser, in reality, Barella? No further information has come to light, but it is curious. (The *Times Picayune* (New Orleans, Louisiana), 6 Nov 1895, p. 7, col. 1, 3).

After three stops in Mississippi, the circus train returned to Bridgeport, Connecticut, with its wagons, tents, tenders, and menagerie. "The show closed at Meridian, Miss., November 9, and its people scattered to all corners of the United States. Quite a party of them went to St. Louis on a special train, among them the bearded lady and her sweetheart."

Since the bearded lady, Annie Jones, and William White (also known by his birth name, William Donovan) had been toddlers, they had been best friends and sweethearts, both having grown up in the Barnum & Bailey. As soon as their ages permitted, they planned to marry. There was, however, a steadfast circus societal rule, which hindered the son of the wardrobe lady (Anna White, widow of William A. Donovan and since 1873, wife of the infamous war hero and lion tamer, Charles Alasco White) from pursuing any romantic attachment to one of the members of the freaks department. It just wasn't done. Although many of the performers were sympathetic to the young pair, Willie's mother held firm in her resolve to keep the couple apart. She carried a lot of weight in the circus and promised to make life very difficult for her son if he married Annie.

As a result, Annie and her beard left the circus for a time and she married another man, Mr. Elliot, a ticket seller. William had then married a seriocomic who had appeared at the White Elephant. Neither of the marriages was successful and soon Annie Jones returned to the Barnum Show and her romance with William rekindled. William's mother, Mrs. Anna White (who claimed she had been with Barnum since 1864) had changed her mind and fully supported the pair. ("Elephant's Dressmaker Defends Her Customers," The *Evening Telegram*, 5 April 1906, p. 18, col. 2–3).

Annie filed for divorce from Elliot in St. Louis through the firm of Bradem & Wood. Papers were filed after Mr. Wood took "dozens of depositions from people connected with the show to support" Annie. The divorce was granted in St. Louis and the couple (with several of their friends) arranged to travel back to New York "on the 3 o'clock fast mail train for the east." It is unknown whether or not this William White (aka Donovan) ever divorced his first wife. The couple's plans included a trip to Europe immediately after the wedding to "fill an engagement in France and Belgium extending over a year."

One-eyed Willie (he had one glass eye) nearly had to wear a patch for his wedding. Friends related that "Willie imbibed a little too freely of the wine when it was red with the result that he lost his "bum eye," as they called it. The artificial optic fell in such a way that a chip was knocked out of it and Willie was in a terrible stew." He was in New York; perhaps it was possible to procure a new "eye" in a hurry.

Mr. White (Donovan) inquired about preachers and marriage licenses at the St. James Hotel in New York the next day. The romantic couple then secured their marriage license and "drove to the residence of a minister where they were married "by a thoroughly perplexed and bewildered pastor." (The *Sunday Herald* (New Haven, Connecticut), 1 Dec 1895, p. 2, col. 5–6).

Mrs. Annie Donovan's (aka Annie Jones married to William White aka Donovan) passport application states that she was born in Marion, Virginia, on 14 July 1865. She called herself a "variety artist." She was traveling to Berlin and Russia. She was thirty-one, 5' 4", had dark brown eyes and hair, prominent nose, medium complexion, a full face and her mouth was "bearded." William A. Donovan (aka William White) professed to being born 26 July 1862 and he called himself a "circus manager." He planned to be on foreign soil for three years. He was thirty-four, 5' 5 and ½" tall, fair complected, sported a mustache, and had dark brown eyes and hair. Although he had less facial hair than his bride, he was one and one half inches taller. Passport applications were filed in Berlin for the couple to continue on to Russia. The actual filing date was 29 December 1896 (National Archives and Records Administration (NARA); Washington D.C.; NARA Series: *Emergency Passport Applications (Issued Abroad), 1877–1907;* Roll #: *36;* Volume #: *Volume 066: Germany*).

The *Times Picayune* of New Orleans reported that "J. A. Bailey, who controls the Barnum & Baidley show and is sole owner of the Adam Forepaugh show, has acquired an interest in the Sells Brother's Circus, and hereafter the Forepaugh and Sells shows will be under the same tent." The intention was to keep the Barnum & Bailey show separate from the "Forepaugh and Sells" show and to have them act as allies, showing in different areas. Bailey had an interest in "Buffalo Bill's Wild West Show," also. (The *Times Picayune* (New Orleans, Louisiana), 29 Nov 1895, p. 7, col. 3). What would 1896 bring?

# — Chapter Fifteen —

*H*ARRY HOUDINI WROTE IN HIS memoirs that Mattie Lee Price faded from the public after separating from her husband and genius lecturer/salesman, W. W. White. Although she was still working in 1895 doing pretty much the same act as she began with in 1884, her name was no longer in the headlines.

The *Western Mail* in South Glamorgan, Whales, advertised an unnamed "Magnetic Lady" in late December 1896 and early January 1897. There is no way of knowing if the dimmed star of Mattie Lee Price was shining in Whales or not. Regardless of where Mattie was working, we did not find her name. There is a good chance that she was again with Barnum & Bailey, at least during the summer.

On February 7, 1897, "Mattie Lee Price, the original Georgia magnetic girl," was scheduled to be at "The Globe" on State Street in Chicago. (The *Chicago Inter Ocean*, 7 Feb 1897, p. 33, col. 5).

During the summer of 1897, Mattie was with "The Great Wallace Shows" out of Cincinnati. She was first listed as "Gaza the Magnetic Girl" in a mid-July advertisement for Sag Harbor, New York. (The *Sag Harbor Express*, 15 July 1897, p.3, col.6). She had bigger, bolder headlines in the Lock Haven, Pennsylvania, advertisement on 2 August. (The *Evening Express*, 2 Aug 1897). She was listed among the performers in advertisements throughout the month of August.

In September, someone finally printed her real name, Mattie Lee Price. She was back in Chicago and would perform at the Clark Street Museum. (The *Chicago Daily Tribune*, 5 Sept 1897, p. 36, col. 3). "David Ellsworth Bates, the self-proclaimed bigamist, will be the stellar feature at the Clark Street Museum for one week longer, after which he will retire from the stage, as he has a pressing engagement for a prolonged stay at the Cook county jail." Showing with Mattie that week were "Charles Johnson, the "half-man" and "Little Egypt," and others. (The *Inter Ocean*, 5 Sept 1897, p. 37, col. 6). Buffalo Bill was in Chicago again, pulling in big crowds at the restored Chicago Coliseum, the very building that had suffered a collapsed roof the year before.

Although "Gaza" was advertised at the Clark Street Museum on 5 September 1897, she was also advertised to be with the Wallace Show that week in Versailles, Indiana. It's a good bet that Mattie made a higher wage at the museum than in the circus and that she "jumped" before advertising for the circus could be pulled. Perhaps the Wallace Show simply decided not to alter the enormous advertisements they used in advance to herald their impending arrival. It is really impossible to know for certain, and not very important. (The *Chicago Daily Tribune*, 5 Sept 1897, p.36, col 3).

Huber's Palace Museum in New York City hosted Mattie Lee Price, the magnetic Georgian (sans "Gaza" moniker) in early November 1897. "The magnetic Georgian presents another style of strength and adds materially in the effectiveness of the bill." (The *New York Clipper*, #594, 6 Nov 1897, col. 3).

Miss M. Price, spinster, departed Liverpool, England, on 10 November 1897 on the steamship Majestic, sister ship of the Teutonic. It could not have been Mattie…or could it? The *Boston Herald* advertised that Mattie Lee Price, the Georgia Marvel, would be at Austin & Stone's Museum the week of November 29. "She is the magnetic phenomenon who has been touring Europe with such great success. This will be her first appearance since her return from abroad." Was Mattie, once again, riding the coattails of a rival's fame? While we know that Annie Abbott had been abroad a great deal in late 1896, we do not know if Mattie was. (*Boston Herald*, 21 Nov 1897, p. 14, col. 2).

That same November, on the twenty-ninth, Annie Abbott's family made headlines for reasons other than her superhuman strength. Annie accused her fourteen-year-old son of stealing her "ring, many loose gems, several bejeweled watches and other valuable trinkets." The boy, Fred, had an accomplice, James Current. The boys went to jail, and Ms. Abbott did not even attend her son's bond hearing. ("Georgia Wonder Robbed," 29 Nov 1897, The *Sun* (Baltimore, Maryland), p. 2, col. 5).

Mattie was getting great hype at Austin & Stone's. There was an interesting, albeit outlandish, article about her every day right up until her last show there on 11 December 1897.

❧

The great manager and showman, James A. Bailey, born on The Fourth of July 1847 and originally named James Anthony McGinnes, made an agreement to take his circus to England in late 1897. He put out a message "notifying all artists and others who desired to remain with the show" to apply for the foreign show before the final Philadelphia show on 9 October 1897.

The tunnels in England were lower than in the United States. All of the circus wagons had to be modified to fit. Alterations in Bridgeport were underway at a frenzied pace that October. "The S. S. Massachusetts which had been selected to transport the show proper reached New York on November 7th." It was a major undertaking to load all of the animals onto the ship. "The led animals such as camels, zebus, zebras, llamas, etc., were walked from the dock… and with the small elephants." It was much different for the full-grown pachyderms. Special cages were constructed that would house them all the way across the Atlantic; and these cages, filled with their enormous occupants, were lifted onto the deck of the boat. It must have looked a little bit like Noah's ark being loaded before the biblical flood. The steamer left the dock on 12 November 1897. On the fifteenth, when Mat MacKay, the giraffe keeper went to "feed his charge, he found the beautiful creature lying in the bottom with her neck broken. She met her death, it is supposed, this way: When about to lie down she turned her head, and the ship, giving a lurch at the moment, threw her off her feet while her head was bent under her." Her name was Daisy and she was 18' feet tall. Two baggage horses and "the high school stallion 'Eagle' also passed on the journey."

The first show of the Barnum & Bailey took place on 27 December 1897 in Olympia, London. It was met with great enthusiasm. We have not been able to verify if Mattie was there for the first show, but we do not find her elsewhere. The *New York Times* (16 Jan 1898, p. 15). mentions, "Scattered here and there are several high and narrow stages, on which the freaks are displayed." An advertisement for the show boasts "3 circus companies combined, 2 Olympic stages and one huge race-track, 2 complete menageries, 3 herds of elephants, museum of living freaks and curiosities, 20 funniest clowns on earth, 70 horses, 2 dreres of camels, hosts of queer animals, 20 races, and 50 trained animals. There were two shows daily and "Menageries, Freak, and Horse Fair departments" could only be opened "from 12 to 4pm and from 6 to 10 pm."

On 28 March 1898 one "Miss Price" arrived in Liverpool, England, on the ship "Numidian" on the Allen Line. Miss Price was single and her profession was "Lady." She was in the "Saloon" part of the ship, or first class. It is doubtful that Mattie would have traveled first class since her name and fame had diminished so greatly, but it is possible that this was her traveling to join, or rejoin, the Greatest Show on Earth at Olympia.

The very first circus parade was given in Manchester, England, on 11 April 1898. The road show would stay in Manchester through the thirtieth. Meanwhile, Annie Abbott was in Bath, England, in mid-June, being her "little Georgia magnet" self.

On 11 June, the *Lichfield Mercury* of Staffordshire, England, provided liberal press for the circus and, more importantly, to the sideshows. Here we find, almost certainly, our own Mattie Lee Price. "The whole show is to be seen for the price paid for admission, the only addition being for the side show, an interesting addition, which is not advertised as an integral part of the exhibition, and yet contains such curiosities as the magnetic lady, the snake charmer, the wild man of Borneo, two diminutive individuals, who lifts very heavy weights, and 'What is it,' is a very peculiar individual." The sideshow included Jo-Jo, the human Skye Terrier or dogface man; the Skeleton Dude,

Herman with his expanding chest who could break chains, Lalloo, the double bodied Hindu boy; and Annie Jones, the bearded lady. The circus production involved "some 860 people." Breakfast was served between 7:00 a.m. and 9:00 a.m. and lunch from 11:30 a.m. to 12:30 p.m. The "love of order" within the circus was noted and appreciated. (The *Lichfield Mercury* (Staffordshire, England) 11 June 1898, p. 11, col. 1). An article that was much the same as the one in the *Lichfield* was printed in the *Yorkshire Evening Post* on 18 June. (The *Yorkshire Evening Post*, 18 June 1898, p. 2, col. 8).

There continued to be other "magnetic ladies" making the rounds in England and Scotland, some of whom began their acts in 1892 when Price and Abbott first arrived. In late August, Madam de Henri was still doing a strong woman act with her husband, Dr. Walford Bodie in Edinburgh at the Pavilion Theatre. (The *Edinburgh Evening News*, 30 August 1898, p. 2, col. 3). West Hartlepool had engaged "Miss Annie May Abbott, the little Georgia magnet, who had appeared at the Alhambra, London, for 140 nights," for the week following 10 September 1898.

# — Chapter Sixteen —

*T*HE TRAVELING CIRCUS BEGAN ON 4 April 1898 at Manchester and ended in Stoke-on-Trent on 12 November. The eclectic conglomeration of tents, equipment, managers, workers, performers, and menagerie had produced their most wonderful extravaganza in seventy different towns and cities in Scotland and England. They were enormously well received by entertainment hungry locals. Performers had a little more than a month to recuperate before the winter season started. (*Four Years in Europe, Barnum & Bailey: The Greatest Show on Earth in the Old World*, Harvey L. Watkins, 1901).

The Luciana, a steamship of the Cunard Line, arrived in Liverpool, England from New York on 1 October 1898. Stepping off that gigantuous ship were two very small, dark haired, blue-eyed children, Jenny and Charles White. Listed as "11" and "8," they appeared to be unaccompanied, although in all fairness they might have had a chaperone. Listed just prior to the children was "Violet Bainbridge," an unmarried girl of seventeen who also seemed to be traveling alone. It is conceivable that "circus kids" might have traveled together to meet up with parents when the circus's road season ended. Jenny and Charles were actually twelve and nine years of age. Could it have been cheaper passage for children twelve and under, therefore motivating someone to understate the children's ages? Mattie would have traveled about four hours by train from London to meet her children in Liverpool and take them back with her.

On December 1, the *Western Mail* (p. 4, col. 7). announced that Bailey had decided to open "Olympia on Boxing Day." He was introducing, an avalanche of new features. Among the new curiosities are Miss Mattie Lee Price, the magnetic wonder; Peter Sampson, the strong man; Great Peter the Small, a midget weighing but 6 ½ pounds; the Orissa Twins, two little girls bound together in a similar manner to the Siamese Twins; Marion Eils, a modeler in soap; Morrell, the Yankee whittler; Master Wade Cochran, a child mental wonder; Sol Stone, the lightening calculator; Miss Belle Carter, a lady with a horse's mane; Karroo, the Congo giant; Albright, a human skeleton; William Wells, the hard-headed man; Professor King, the paper king, and Okabe, a Japanese armless lady.

The talking dog, educated pigs, and cat orchestra were coming, too. Forty freaks were on their way to London on the steamer, S.

S. Manitou in late November. (The S.S. Manitou made its maiden voyage just ten months earlier). And although Mattie was listed as one of the freaks on that ship, she was already in London getting to know her children.

There was a wonderful sketch posted in the *Westminster Budget* (London, Middlesex) on 16 December depicting all of the new freaks (and the old ones) who could be expected at the Barnum & Bailey Greatest Show on Earth at Olympia on Boxing Day. ("Barnum and Bailey. Greatest Show on Earth," The *Westminster Budget*, 16 Dec 1898, p. 4).

The *Era*, (London, England, 17 Dec 1898, p. 23, col. 1). had a full column write-up about the coming curious attractions at Olympia. Laloo and Lala were billed as "brother and sister." The parasitic half-twin (Lala) was billed as the brother and Laloo, the host twin, was billed as his sister, even though he was, of course, male. It made things more "curious," you see. Both Mattie Lee Price and Annie Jones were respectfully mentioned.

"Freaks in Revolt" led the headlines of the *Daily News* (7 Jan 1899, p. 8, col. 4). and a similar article ran in the *London Times* on the same day ("The 'Freaks of Olympia'" The *London Times*, 7 Jan 1899, p. 6, col. 1). Apparently, Annie Jones, the bearded lady (married to one-eyed Willie, only son of the wardrobe lady), led the discussion in a meeting held to address the problem of the misnomer, "freaks." Everyone from the freak department "raised their hands" in agreement that the word should be abandoned, except for, of course, "Tripp and Oguri" who were armless.

All of the so-called-freaks at the meeting eventually agreed that the word "freaks" should be replaced with the word "prodigies" in the future. Signing the declaration for change were thirty-four persons of the freak department, including Mattie Lee Price. (*The Era* (London, England), 14 Jan 1899, p. 19, col. 5). "This committee in fulfillment of their mission presented themselves at the Managers Office, were courteously received by Mr. Bailey, who listened to their statement and immediately gave instructions that all signs be at once changed substituting the new word and that in future all publications should refer to them only by the new title." (*Four Years in Europe, Barnum & Bailey: The Greatest Show on Earth in the Old World*, Harvey L. Watkins, 1901, p. 22).

The hullabaloo about the respectable renaming of the freak department generated a lot of press in England as well as overseas and "patronage continued good throughout the month of January." One can speculate that the "freak" issue was addressed for the sole purpose of generating publicity. A visitor was required to pay extra to see the "prodigies," because that department was not included in the circus entry fee. The circus put out a brand-new poster embracing the renaming of the freak department. "The Peerless Prodigies of Physical Phenomena and Great Presentation of Marvelous Living Human Curiosities.

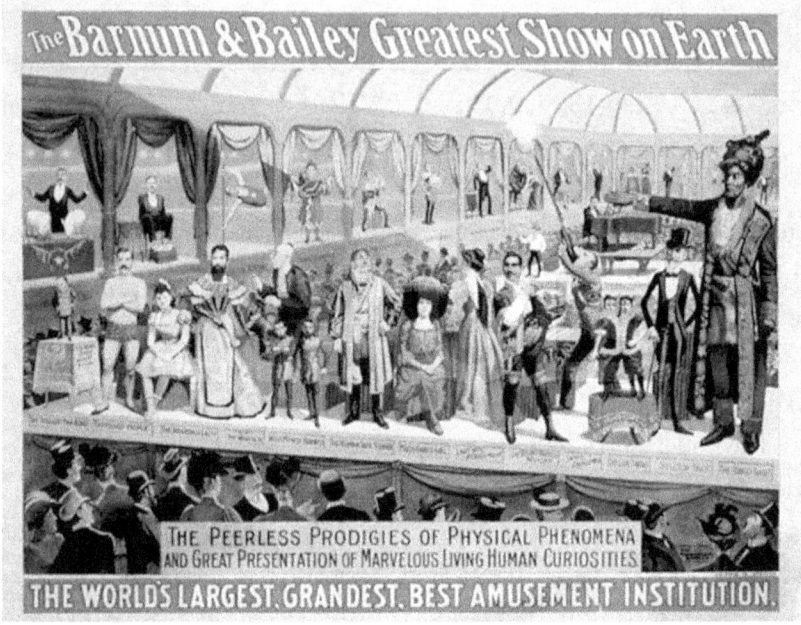

Mattie Lee Price appears 8th from left on the raised stages.

In February there was a nice stateside write-up about the success of the American show in London, and within that article is a note about Mattie. "Strength and skill probably account for the feats of Mattie Lee Price—with perhaps a dash of nature thrown in. How otherwise can you account for this 'charming, delicate, womanly woman lifting from the ground by the mere touch of her hand a chair loaded with three stalwart men?'" (The *Iowa City Press-Citizen* (Iowa City, Iowa), 24 Feb 1899, p. 2).

The Official Barnum & Bailey Limited photograph of Mattie was taken on 4 March 1899 at 3 Crosby Square, London, E.C., by photographer James Ernest Hunt and is held in the National Archives. The photograph description reads, "Photograph of Mattie Lee Price, the Magnetic Wonder lifting 4 men in a chair."

Mattie Lee Price

There was a rare profile photograph and short article about Mattie in the *Sketch, a Journal of Art and Actuality*, volume XXIV, which covered 26 October 1898 through 18 January of 1899. (Ingram Brothers, 198 Strand, London 28 December 1898, p. 338). "Not all the freaks of Olympia are natural abnormalities; about half are artificial. That is to say, some of the curiosities have made themselves what they are; the others were made such by the whim of Nature." Of Mattie in particular they said, "Strength *and* skill probably account for the feats of Mattie Lee Price—with perhaps a dash of Nature thrown in. How otherwise can you account for this 'charming, delicate, womanly woman (vide the Barnum and Bailey advertisements) lifting from the ground by the mere touch of her hand a chair loaded with three stalwart men?'" Here she was named "The Georgia Electric Wonder."

Mattie Lee Price

On the same page with Mattie in the Sketch were descriptions of Skeleton Dude, the Albino Distortionist, and Billy Wells, also known as the "Hard Head Man."

Mattie's description was identical to an article printed in the 24 Febrary 1899 *Iowa City Press-Citizen*, and almost certainly the official Barnum & Bailey promotional text.

On 11 March 1899, Mattie Lee Price passed away at number 81 Hammersmith Road, Fulham District, London, England.

The death certificate recorded her name as "Mattie Lee Aronson." She had suffered a miscarriage eleven days prior and "cellulitis and septicemia" were the cause of death.

Louis Aronson was listed as "widower of deceased and was present upon her death." Under Mattie's occupation was written, "Wife of Louis Aronson, Lecturer on Human Curiosities." So it seems that even though Mattie was the breadwinner and Aronson only the promoter, her occupation was minimalistically recorded as "wife of…" a man. Those were the times she lived in.

And, although the official document of death filled in by "R. Bevan, LRCP," records Mattie as being 30 years of age, she would never cross that threshold; her birthday was still two months away.

Mattie Lee Aronson Death Record

*Lloyd's Weekly* wrote, "The Greatest Show on Earth has suffered the loss of its 'Magnetic Wonder,' Mrs. Mattie Price, who has succumbed to a sharp attack of peritonitis at the early age of 32 years. Deceased was a popular member of the freak department." (London, England, 19 March 1899). "Her funeral was attended by a great many of our people and the remains were laid away in Hammersmith cemetery. (*Four Years in Europe, Barnum & Bailey: The Greatest Show on Earth in the Old World*, Harvey L. Watkins, p.22, 1901).

The officiating minister was Geo. String. The grave location was section 8, row E, number 22. The unconsecrated gravesite was 5' 8" long and 1' 5" wide and was owned by George R Earsdon of 129 Shepherds Bush Road. The funeral took place on 13 March at 2:30 p.m. (Records of Fulham Old Burial Ground in Fulham Palace Road. Reference 2012/05746).

What happened to Mattie's children? Did they attend their mother's funeral? Had they gazed upon her face as she slept her eternal sleep?

Undoubtedly, the plan had been for the children to stay with their mother as the circus played in England and then crossed the channel to Europe. They had grown old enough to accompany her, just in time for her to leave them again forever.

We know that Jenny and Charles White were counted in the 1900 census in Lena, Wisconsin, as boarders within the Riffle household. How they went from London to Lena is still a mystery.

# — Afterword —

*T*HE MARKERS ON THE GRAVES in the Old Fultham Cemetery have been vandalized and so there is no marker for Mattie Lee Price. Let this book be a marker to remember her by.

The process of uncovering the truth about my great-grandmother, has been more than a research project, it has been a journey of my own soul. Memories stirred are not always sweet but both good and bad experiences are what we are ultimately made of. It is the difficult times that grow us strong, so we must be grateful for them.

I absolutely hated Mattie's father, George Washington Price, for taking Mattie on the road at the tender age of fourteen, especially in a time when women had few rights and were supposed to be retiring and modest. While teenaged girls believe they know everything, they most certainly do not. They need guidance and someone to make sure they don't color outside the lines of decency and mess up their lives. This loathing of George Price inspired me to research his past further, and as a result I am humbled.

George was born in northern Georgia on 3 June 1847. His parents, William E. Price and Alvira Ann (Burks) Price, owned a farm in Murray County. When the War Between the States broke out in 1861, they were supporting themselves and eleven children on that land.

Since George's father was under forty-five at the time, he would have been required to enlist in the Confederate army, but he never did. He stayed on the farm. Having someone serve in your "stead," was a common practice during the Civil War. Since George was only fourteen and not legally required to enlist, he probably served in his father's "stead." No one could have dreamed that the Civil War would last so long or be so bloody.

George joined the 36th Infantry Regiment on 1 Feb 1862 in Dalton, Georgia, a short distance from the farm. His regiment was trapped in the Siege of Vicksburg, and he surrendered to General Grant's troops on 4 July 1863. Because there was no possible way for the Union army to imprison and feed the Confederate prisoners, they were released. The prisoners only had to sign a document swearing they would never take up arms against the Union again, and they were let go. George signed his name with an "x." The consensus was that the Confederate captives were so emotionally broken, they would never have the heart to fight again. This, of course, was faulty logic, as the southern boys began to fight again as soon as they were released.

On 3 June 1864, whether or not he was aware of it at the time, George's older brother, Henry, who was in Company E, 4th Battalion (Stiles) 60th Regiment of the Georgia infantry, was killed in battle at Cold Harbor, Virginia. It was George's seventeenth birthday.

George Price was recaptured near Marietta, Georgia, on 12 July 1864 and transferred to a military prison at Louisville, Kentucky.

From there he was transferred to Camp Douglas in Chicago, Illinois, on 17 July. On 3 April 1865, while at Camp Douglas, he enlisted in the 6th US Volunteers for a stint of three years. He could not have known the Civil War would end just 15 days later, on 18 April. If he had held off signing up for another two weeks, he could have gone home. Union records give his description as sixteen years of age, born in Morris, Georgia, gray eyes, "5 foot and 5 and a quarter inches" and a farmer. He was actually close to eighteen. He, like Mattie, was good at telling "stories."

He spent April through September of 1865 in the camp hospital at Fort Douglas. No malady was described. In December of that same year he was marked absent, dispatched to the quartermaster department as teamster, where he probably drove horses to deliver supplies. January 1866 he was in the same detail, but sent to "Post Cottonwood, NT," Nebraska Territory. March of 1866 he was listed as a company cook, but then he was off again as an escort with a surveying party April through July of 1866.

George deserted his post in Denver, Colorado, 23 August 1866. Federal documents record that he took with him one Springfield Rifle Musket.58 caliber worth $19.25 along with his bayonet, scabbard, cap, screwdriver, cartridge box and belt, waist belt and plane, a cone wrench, great coat, hat with bugles and number, knapsack, haversack, and canteen. The "store's lost" to this deserter were listed as $23.62.

He made his way back to Georgia and married Rhoda McAbee in northern Georgia in 1868. They produced three children, Mattie, the eldest, and migrated to Arkansas. In some unknown tragedy around 1874, George lost them all except Mattie.

George Washington Price had survived going to war at fourteen and the loss of his older brother, Henry. He lost his young wife and two of their babies before his thirtieth birthday. He probably believed it was not too much to ask to have his fourteen-year-old daughter put on a pretty dress, and go on stage to make more money in one year than he cleared in three. Besides, Mattie would no longer be required to work on the farm or tend the children at home. It was a different time with different circumstances.

George and his second wife, Elizabeth Price, moved their extended family to Texas sometime before the 1900 census, where they were listed in Justice Precinct 6, Van Zandt County. Elizabeth stated she had one deceased child and Georgia was missing from the household. Mattie's father is buried in the Simpsonville Cemetery near Thomas in Upshur, County, Texas. He died in 1917. You can only read his name when the sun shines on the headstone just right. I understand better now.

We do not have records of Mattie's fourth marriage to Louis Aronson. In 1907, a man we believe was the same Louis Aronson listed on Mattie's death certificate, who was a former "side show manager," bought and opened a theater in Baraboo, Wisconsin. The man, "Lew Aronson," remodeled a building at 142 Third Street to make it a vaudeville and moving picture theater. (Images of Baraboo, Sauk County Historical Society, Arcadia Publishing, ISBN 978-0-7385-3299-8, p. 69).

Of Louis Barella, Mattie's third husband, we believe he was the same man listed as "ticket seller" with the 1901 Ringling Brother's Circus and again in 1905 as sideshow manager with the Campbell Brothers. (Billboard, 25 Feb 1905, p. 10–11).

Of William W. White, we have no further information past 1893 when Mattie and he parted ways—that is, other than a family memory about someone saying he had been somewhere in Texas. And after processing two different DNA tests from Charles Joseph White's grandson, it appears that William White was, in all probability, not the father of Mattie's son. That would explain why the orphaned children went to the Riffles in Wisconsin and not to White after their mother died.

Charles Joseph White on far left. His wife Nora second from right.

Of Samuel Wise, Mattie's first husband, we have no information as to his beginning or end. DNA testing does not reveal any close "Wise" relatives to Jenny's grandchildren and there is only a trace of "European Jewish" heritage found. We believe Mattie was already expecting Jenny when she married him.

The Price connection with DNA is strong for both Charles White's descendants and Jenny's. A great-granddaughter of one of Mattie's half-sisters (Emma, born in 1884) lives in East Texas and provided the very young photo of Mattie that looks like a coaster with a torn corner. It is not labeled. She found it among the familial photos left behind, and we believe it is Mattie.

Mattie Lee Price ~ 1884

Quite by accident (or was it?) the middle name of "Lee" has flowed down through the generations, and Mattie has a great-granddaughter, a second great-granddaughter, and third great-granddaughter who all share that middle name. The youngest is, of course, fourteen. Was Mattie's middle name to honor General Robert E. Lee?

Mattie, and probably her mother, Rhoda McAbee, were less than thirty years old when they perished. What an incredibly random act of nature that any of our unique selves make it into this world! Either it's chance or we are simply meant to be.

# — The Last Word —

*I* CLOSE MY EYES AND I am six years old, standing on a grassy hillside in the early summer sunshine. The circus parade is coming, and I hear the raspy notes of the calliope drawing closer. Walking behind the first few brightly colored wagons is a group of performers, aerialists, acrobats, and clowns. I see her and I raise my hand to wave, and she looks me right in the eye, smiles quietly, and waves. The tears flow freely from my little girl eyes as I realize, I finally found her—my circus grandma.

# — About the Author —

Donna Lee (Riffle) Dicksson lives in Garland, Texas with her naturalized Swedish husband, Peter and two parrots. She was born in Idaho and grew up in western Montana.

One of the first things she confided to her new husband in 1990 was her "unusual center of gravity." At 120 pounds, she easily lifted his 240 pounds straight up off of the floor. It was not until 2012 that she uncovered the name and occupation of Mattie Lee Price, undoubtedly the genetic source of her lifting capabilities.

Happy, lucky, grandma with a camera, Donna has two children, three granddaughters, and one great granddaughter. She is both a volunteer and professional photographer and plans many more research projects and books.

www.Dicksson.Com
Donna@Dicksson.com